D1298882

THAI

p

This is a Parragon Book
This edition published in 2005

Parragon
Queen Street House
4 Queen Street
Bath BA1 1HE, UK

Copyright © Parragon 2004

1-40544-862-8

Printed in China

Produced by the Bridgewater Book Company Ltd.

NOTE

This book uses metric and imperial measurements. Follow the same
units of measurement throughout; do not mix metric and imperial.
All spoon measurements are level: teaspoons are assumed to be 5 ml,
and tablespoons are assumed to be 15 ml. Unless otherwise stated,
milk is assumed to be full fat, eggs and individual vegetables such as
potatoes are medium, and pepper is freshly ground black pepper.

The times given for each recipe are an approximate guide only,
because the cooking times may vary as a result of the types of
oven and other equipment used.

Recipes using raw or very lightly cooked eggs should be
avoided by infants, the elderly, pregnant women, convalescents
and anyone suffering from an illness. Pregnant and breast-feeding
women are advised to avoid eating peanuts and peanut products.

Contents

Introduction

Anyone who loves Thai food will appreciate that it is a unique cuisine, distinctly different from the cooking of the countries which border it, but with many culinary influences from far beyond its geographical frontiers. Thai cooking owes many of its characteristics to climate and culture, but a

history of many centuries of invasions and emigration has played a large part in shaping its cuisine. The roots of the Thai nation can be traced back to the first century A.D., the time of the Chinese Han Dynasty, when the T'ai tribes occupied parts of South China along valuable trade routes between the East and West. Over the years, the T'ai had a close but often stormy relationship with the Chinese, and eventually began to emigrate south to the lands of what is now northern Thailand, bordering Burma and Cambodia, then sparsely occupied by Buddhist and Hindu communities.

In time, the T'ai established the independent Kingdom of Sukhothai (translated as 'dawn of happiness'), which eventually became Siam. The ports of Siam were the entrance to an important trade route, and ships from all over Europe and Japan docked there, or sailed inland along the rivers, bringing foreign foods, teas, spices, silks, copper and ceramics. In the 16th century, the Portuguese introduced the chilli to Southeast Asia. The plant flourished immediately in the region's soils and climates, and continues to thrive. Trade with Arab and Indian merchants was important, and many Muslims settled in Siam.

Siam became the Kingdom of Thailand in 1939 after a period of political upheaval, and twenty-first-century Thailand still reflects much of her past centuries of mixed culture, witnessed by the independence, creativity and passion of the nation. This love of life is apparent in the way they take pleasure in

entertaining and eating. To a visitor they seem to eat all day long. The streets and waterways are lined with food vendors selling a huge variety of tasty snacks from their stalls, carts, bicycles and boats.

Parties and celebrations are extremely popular, and during the many festivals, the colourful, often elaborate and carefully prepared festive foods show a respect for custom and tradition. Visitors are entertained with an unending succession of trays of tasty snacks, platters of exotic fruits, and Thai beer or local whisky. When a meal is served, all the dishes are served together, so the cook can enjoy the food along with the guests.

Presenting food beautifully is a source of great pride in Thailand. Vegetables and fruits are sometimes carved into elaborate shapes for use as garnishes — intricate patterns and skilled artistry are an integral part of Thai culture, which exhibits a deep appreciation of all things beautiful.

Everyday life in Thailand is closely tied to the seasons, marked by the harvesting of crops and the vagaries of the monsoon climate. Food is taken seriously, with great care taken in choosing the freshest of ingredients, and thoughtfully balancing delicate flavours and textures. Throughout Thailand, rice is the most important staple food, the centre of every meal. And coconut, in its various forms, has an almost equal place. Cooks in every region are expert at making the most of any ingredient available locally, so the character of many classic Thai dishes will vary according to the region in which they are cooked.

5

Fundamentals of Thai Cooking

The essential ingredients you need in order to cook Thai food are listed here. Of these, the most important are coconut, lime, chilli, rice, garlic, lemon grass, root ginger and coriander. With these you can create many traditional Thai dishes. Although many recipes have long lists of ingredients, the cooking methods involved in making them are simple enough even for inexperienced cooks to follow.

Balance is the guiding principle of Thai cooking, the five extremes of flavour – bitter, sour, hot, salty and sweet – being carefully and skilfully balanced in each dish and over several courses. Every dish therefore contributes to the balance of the entire meal.

Basil
Three varieties of sweet basil are used in Thai cooking, but the variety commonly sold in the West also works well. Asian food shops often sell the seeds for Thai basil, so you can grow your own.

Chillies
The many varieties of chilli vary in heat from very mild to fiery hot, so choose carefully. The small red or green bird's eye chillies are often used in Thai dishes. They are very hot, and if you prefer a mild heat you should remove the seeds. Red chillies are generally slightly sweeter and milder than green ones. Larger chillies tend to be milder. Dried crushed chillies are used for seasoning.

Coconut Milk
This is made from grated, pressed fresh coconut. It is sold very widely in cans and longlife packs, in powdered form, and in blocks as creamed coconut. Coconut cream is skimmed from the top, and is slightly thicker and richer.

Coriander
This is a herb with a pungent, citrus-like flavour, widely used in savoury dishes. It wilts quite quickly, so retains its freshness best if bought with a root

6

attached. Alternatively, you can grow your own. It will make your cooking taste even better.

Galangal
A relative of ginger, with a milder, aromatic flavour. It is available fresh or dried.

Garlic
The pungent cloves of this bulb are used abundantly in Thai cooking. It is used whole, crushed, sliced or chopped in savoury dishes and curry pastes. Pickled garlic is a useful ingredient to have in the storecupboard because it makes an attractive garnish.

Ginger
Fresh root ginger is peeled and grated, chopped or sliced for a warm, spicy flavour.

Kaffir Lime Leaves
These leaves have a distinctive lime scent, and can be bought fresh, dried or frozen.

Lemon Grass
An aromatic tropical grass with a lemon scent similar to lemon balm. Strip off the fibrous outer leaves and slice or chop the insides finely, or bruise and use whole. It can also be bought in dried, powdered form.

Palm Sugar
This is a rich, brown, unrefined sugar made from the coconut palm and sold in blocks. The best way to use it is to crush it with a mallet. Muscovado sugar is a good substitute.

Rice Vinegar
Mirin, or sweet rice vinegar, is a savoury flavouring. Sherry or white wine vinegar can be substituted.

Soy Sauce
Dark and light soy sauce are used for seasoning. The light sauce is saltier than the dark and is used in stir-fries and with light meats. Dark soy adds a rich flavour and colour to braised and red meat dishes.

Tamarind Paste
The pulp of the tamarind fruit is usually sold in blocks. It gives a sour/sweet flavour. Soak the pulp in a bowl of hot water for 30 minutes, then press out the juice and discard the pulp and seeds.

Thai Curry Paste
This flavouring varies in heat, with yellow the mildest, red variable and green the hottest.

Thai Fish Sauce
Called nam pla, this is used like salt for seasoning savoury dishes, and has a distinctive, intense aroma.

Soups

Soups are part of almost every Thai meal, including breakfast. Lunch is often a large bowl of soup – a thin stock-based broth, usually spiked with fresh red or green chillies, and with the addition of fine noodles, rice, egg strips or tiny fish balls, and meat balls or cubes of tofu. In restaurants, soups are often served in a large 'firepot' with a central funnel of burning coals to keep the contents hot.

The soups featured in this section are perfect for any time of the day and whatever the occasion, whether it is a formal dinner party or a summer barbecue lunch. They all use traditional Thai ingredients, and the most typical ones can be easily found in Thai food shops and supermarkets.

chilli-spiced prawn wonton soup

serves four

WONTONS

175 g/6 oz cooked peeled prawns

1 garlic clove, crushed

1 spring onion, finely chopped

1 tbsp dark soy sauce

1 tbsp Thai fish sauce

1 tbsp chopped fresh coriander

1 small egg, separated

12 wonton wrappers

SOUP

2 small fresh red bird's eye chillies

2 spring onions

1 litre/1¾ pints clear beef stock

1 tbsp Thai fish sauce

1 tbsp dark soy sauce

1 tbsp rice wine or dry sherry

handful of fresh coriander leaves,
  to garnish

1 Finely chop the prawns. Place them in a bowl and stir in the garlic, spring onion, soy sauce, fish sauce, coriander and egg yolk.

2 Lay the wonton wrappers on a work surface in a single layer and place about 1 tablespoon of the filling mixture in the centre of each. Brush the edges with egg white and fold each one into a triangle, pressing lightly to seal. Bring the 2 bottom corners of the triangle around to meet in the middle, securing with a little egg white to hold in place.

3 To make the soup, slice the chillies at a steep diagonal angle to make long thin slices. Slice the spring onions on the same angle.

4 Place the stock, fish sauce, soy sauce and rice wine in a large saucepan and bring to the boil. Add the chillies and spring onions. Drop the wontons into the saucepan and simmer for 4–5 minutes, or until thoroughly heated.

5 Serve the soup and wontons in small bowls and garnish with coriander at the last moment.

10

rice soup with eggs

serves four

1 tsp sunflower oil

1 garlic clove, crushed

50 g/1¾ oz minced pork

3 spring onions, sliced

1 tbsp grated fresh root ginger

1 fresh red bird's eye chilli,
    deseeded and chopped

1 litre/1¾ pints chicken stock

200 g/7 oz cooked long-grain rice

1 tbsp Thai fish sauce

salt and pepper

4 small eggs

2 tbsp shredded fresh coriander,
    to garnish

1 Heat the oil in a large saucepan or preheated wok.

2 Add the garlic and pork and stir-fry gently for 1 minute, or until the meat is broken up but not browned.

3 Add the spring onions, ginger, chilli and stock, stirring until boiling. Add the rice, reduce the heat and simmer for 2 minutes.

4 Add the fish sauce and season to taste with salt and pepper. Carefully break the eggs into the soup and simmer over a very low heat for 3–4 minutes, or until set.

5 Ladle the soup into large bowls, allowing 1 egg per portion. Garnish with shredded coriander and serve immediately.

COOK'S TIP

If you prefer, beat the eggs together and fry like an omelette until set, then cut into ribbon-like strips and add to the soup just before serving.

tom yam gung

serves four

450 ml/16 fl oz light chicken stock

2 fresh kaffir lime leaves, chopped

5-cm/2-inch piece lemon
grass, chopped

3 tbsp lemon juice

3 tbsp Thai fish sauce

2 small hot green chillies, deseeded
and finely chopped

1 tsp sugar

8 small shiitake mushrooms or
8 straw mushrooms, halved

450 g/1 lb raw prawns, peeled if
necessary and deveined

spring onion strips, to garnish

TOM YAM SAUCE

4 tbsp vegetable oil

5 garlic cloves, finely chopped

1 large shallot, finely chopped

2 large hot dried red chillies,
roughly chopped

1 tbsp dried shrimp (optional)

1 tbsp Thai fish sauce

2 tsp sugar

1 First make the tom yam sauce. Heat the oil in a saucepan. Add the garlic and cook for a few seconds until the garlic just browns. Remove with a slotted spoon and reserve. Add the shallot to the same oil and fry until browned and crisp. Remove with a slotted spoon and reserve. Add the chillies and fry until they darken. Remove from the oil and drain on kitchen paper. Remove the saucepan from the heat and reserve the oil.

2 Grind the dried shrimp, if using, in a food processor or spice grinder, then add the reserved chillies, garlic and shallots. Grind to a smooth paste. Return the saucepan with the original oil to a low heat, add the paste and warm through. Add the fish sauce and sugar and mix. Remove the saucepan from the heat.

3 Heat the stock and 2 tablespoons of the tom yam sauce together in a separate saucepan. Add the lime leaves, lemon grass, lemon juice, fish sauce, chillies and sugar and simmer for 2 minutes.

4 Add the mushrooms and prawns and cook for a further 2–3 minutes, or until the prawns are cooked. Ladle into warmed serving bowls and serve immediately, garnished with spring onion strips.

thai-style seafood soup

serves four

1.2 litres/2 pints fish stock

1 lemon grass stalk,
  split lengthways

pared rind of ½ lime or 1 fresh
  kaffir lime leaf

2.5-cm/1-inch piece fresh root
  ginger, sliced

¼ tsp chilli purée, or to taste

4–6 spring onions

200 g/7 oz large or medium raw
  prawns, peeled

salt

250 g/9 oz scallops (16–20)

2 tbsp fresh coriander leaves

finely chopped red pepper, or fresh
  red chilli rings, to garnish

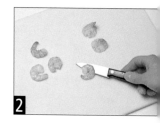

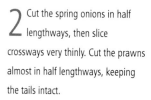

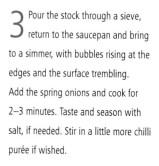

1 Place the stock in a saucepan with the lemon grass, lime rind, ginger and chilli purée. Bring just to the boil, reduce the heat, cover and simmer for 10–15 minutes.

2 Cut the spring onions in half lengthways, then slice crossways very thinly. Cut the prawns almost in half lengthways, keeping the tails intact.

3 Pour the stock through a sieve, return to the saucepan and bring to a simmer, with bubbles rising at the edges and the surface trembling. Add the spring onions and cook for 2–3 minutes. Taste and season with salt, if needed. Stir in a little more chilli purée if wished.

4 Add the scallops and prawns and poach for 1 minute, or until they turn opaque and the prawns curl.

5 Drop in the fresh coriander leaves, ladle the soup into warmed serving bowls, dividing the shellfish evenly, and garnish with chopped red pepper or chilli rings.

VARIATION

If you have light chicken stock, but no fish stock, it will make an equally tasty though different version of this soup.

hot & sour soup

serves four

350 g/12 oz whole raw or cooked
    prawns in shells

1 tbsp vegetable oil

1 lemon grass stalk,
    roughly chopped

2 fresh kaffir lime leaves, shredded

1 fresh green chilli, deseeded
    and chopped

1.2 litres/2 pints chicken or
    fish stock

1 lime

1 tbsp Thai fish sauce

salt and pepper

1 fresh red bird's eye chilli,
    deseeded and thinly sliced

1 spring onion, thinly sliced

1 tbsp finely chopped fresh
    coriander, to garnish

COOK'S TIP

To devein the prawns, remove
the shells. Cut a slit along the
back of each prawn and remove
the fine black vein that runs
along the length of the back.
Wipe with kitchen paper.

1 Peel the prawns and reserve the shells. Devein the prawns (see Cook's Tip), then cover with clingfilm and leave to chill in the refrigerator.

2 Heat the oil in a large, heavy-based saucepan. Add the prawn shells and stir-fry for 3–4 minutes, or until they turn pink. Add the lemon grass, lime leaves, chilli and stock. Pare a thin strip of rind from the lime and grate the rest. Add the grated rind to the saucepan.

3 Bring to the boil, then reduce the heat, cover and leave to simmer for 20 minutes.

4 Sieve the liquid and pour it back into the saucepan. Squeeze the juice from the lime and add to the saucepan with the fish sauce and salt and pepper to taste.

5 Bring to the boil, then reduce the heat and add the prawns. Simmer for 2–3 minutes.

6 Add the thinly sliced chilli and spring onion. Sprinkle with the chopped coriander and serve.

chicken noodle soup

serves four–six

1 sheet dried egg noodles from a
  250 g/9 oz packet

1 tbsp sunflower oil

4 skinless, boneless chicken
  thighs, diced

1 bunch of spring onions, sliced

2 garlic cloves, chopped

2-cm/¾-inch piece fresh root ginger,
  finely chopped

850 ml/1½ pints chicken stock

200 ml/7 fl oz coconut milk

3 tsp Thai red curry paste

3 tbsp peanut butter

2 tbsp light soy sauce

salt and pepper

1 small red pepper, deseeded
  and chopped

55 g/2 oz frozen peas

VARIATION

You can use other types
of noodles in this soup, such
as rice or cellophane noodles.
Prepare according to the
packet instructions.

1 Place the noodles in a shallow heatproof dish and leave to soak in boiling water according to the packet instructions.

2 Heat the oil in a large, heavy-based saucepan or preheated wok. Add the chicken and stir-fry for 5 minutes, or until lightly browned. Add the white part of the spring onions, the garlic and ginger and stir-fry for 2 minutes.

3 Add the stock, coconut milk, curry paste, peanut butter and soy sauce. Season to taste with salt and pepper. Bring to the boil, stirring constantly, then simmer for 8 minutes, stirring occasionally. Add the red pepper, peas and green spring onion tops and cook for a further 2 minutes.

4 Add the drained noodles and heat through. Spoon into warmed serving bowls and serve immediately.

16

chicken & coconut milk soup

serves four

400 ml/14 fl oz canned
   coconut milk

500 ml/18 fl oz chicken stock

6 thin slices fresh galangal

2 stalks lemon grass, bruised

4 fresh kaffir lime leaves

225 g/8 oz chicken breast fillets

4 spring onions

2 fresh red chillies, deseeded and
   finely sliced

4 tbsp Thai fish sauce

2 tbsp lime juice

2 tbsp chopped fresh coriander

1 Place the coconut milk, stock, galangal, lemon grass and lime leaves in a large saucepan and bring to the boil.

2 Cut the chicken into strips and add to the saucepan. Reduce the heat and simmer for 10 minutes, or until the chicken is cooked.

3 Slice the spring onions and add to the saucepan with the chillies. Simmer for a further 3 minutes. Stir in the fish sauce, lime juice and coriander and serve in warmed bowls.

18

spicy thai soup with prawns

serves four

2 tbsp tamarind paste

4 fresh red bird's eye chillies, very
   finely chopped

2 garlic cloves, crushed

2.5-cm/1-inch piece galangal, very
   finely chopped

4 tbsp Thai fish sauce

2 tbsp palm sugar or caster sugar

8 fresh kaffir lime leaves,
   roughly torn

1.2 litres/2 pints fish stock

100 g/3½ oz carrots, very
   thinly sliced

350 g/12 oz sweet potato, diced

100 g/3½ oz baby corn cobs, halved

3 tbsp fresh coriander,
   roughly chopped

100 g/3½ oz cherry
   tomatoes, halved

225 g/8 oz fantail prawns

1 Place the tamarind paste, chillies, garlic, galangal, fish sauce, sugar, lime leaves and stock in a large, preheated wok. Bring to the boil, stirring constantly.

2 Reduce the heat and add the carrots, sweet potato and baby corn cobs to the mixture in the wok.

COOK'S TIP

Galangal or Thai ginger is a member of the ginger family, but it is yellow in colour with pink sprouts. The flavour is aromatic and less pungent than ginger.

3 Leave the soup to simmer, uncovered, for 10 minutes, or until the vegetables are just tender.

4 Stir the coriander, cherry tomatoes and prawns into the soup and heat through for 5 minutes.

5 Transfer the soup to warmed serving bowls and serve hot.

mushroom & tofu broth

serves four

4 dried shiitake mushrooms

150 ml/5 fl oz boiling water

1 tbsp sunflower oil

1 tsp sesame oil

1 garlic clove, crushed

1 fresh green chilli, deseeded and
finely chopped

6 spring onions, sliced

85 g/3 oz oyster mushrooms, sliced

2 fresh kaffir lime leaves,
finely shredded

1 litre/1¾ pints rich brown stock

2 tbsp lime juice

1 tbsp rice vinegar or white
wine vinegar

1 tbsp Thai fish sauce

85 g/3 oz firm tofu (drained weight),
diced

salt and pepper

1 Place the dried shiitake mushrooms in a heatproof bowl and pour over the boiling water. Leave to soak for 30 minutes. Drain, reserving the liquid, then roughly chop the mushrooms.

2 Heat the sunflower and sesame oils in a large saucepan or preheated wok over a high heat. Add the garlic, chilli and spring onions and stir-fry for 1 minute, or until softened but not browned.

3 Add all of the mushrooms, lime leaves, stock and reserved mushroom liquid. Bring to the boil.

4 Stir in the lime juice, rice vinegar and fish sauce, then reduce the heat and leave to simmer gently for 3–4 minutes.

5 Add the diced tofu and season to taste with salt and pepper. Heat gently until boiling, then ladle into warmed serving bowls and serve.

COOK'S TIP

Use a clear, richly coloured home-made beef stock, or a Japanese dashi, to make an attractive clear broth. Stock cubes generally make a cloudy stock. To make a vegetarian version of the broth, use a well-flavoured vegetable stock and replace the fish sauce with light soy sauce.

20

aromatic chicken & vegetable soup

serves four

½ lime

handful of fresh coriander

1 litre/1¾ pints chicken stock

1 lemon grass stalk, bruised

1 small fresh red chilli

salt and pepper

225 g/8 oz skinless, boneless
   chicken breasts

1 carrot

100 g/3½ oz mangetout, cut into
   thin diagonal strips

100 g/3½ oz baby corn cobs,
   thinly sliced

4 spring onions, thinly sliced

1 Grate the lime. Strip the coriander leaves from the stalks. Reserve the leaves and place the stalks in a saucepan with the stock, lemon grass, chilli and lime rind. Bring to the boil, then cover and simmer for 15 minutes.

2 Sieve the stock into a separate saucepan. Squeeze in the lime juice, and add salt and pepper to taste.

3 Dice the chicken and add to the stock. Bring to the boil, then simmer for 5 minutes. Cut the carrot into ribbons and add to the saucepan with the mangetout and corn. Simmer for 2 minutes, or until the vegetables are tender and the chicken is cooked.

4 Roughly chop the coriander leaves and stir into the soup with the spring onions. Serve immediately.

21

chilled avocado, lime & coriander soup

serves four

2 ripe avocados

1 small mild onion, chopped

1 garlic clove, crushed

2 tbsp chopped fresh coriander

1 tbsp chopped fresh mint

2 tbsp lime juice

700 ml/1¼ pints vegetable stock

1 tbsp rice vinegar or white
    wine vinegar

1 tbsp light soy sauce

salt and pepper

TO GARNISH

2 tbsp soured cream

1 tbsp finely chopped
    fresh coriander

2 tsp lime juice

finely shredded lime rind

1 Halve, stone and scoop out the flesh from the avocados. Place in a food processor or blender with the onion, garlic, coriander, mint, lime juice and about half the stock and process until completely smooth.

2 Add the remaining stock, rice vinegar and soy sauce and process again to mix well. Taste and adjust the seasoning if necessary, or add a little extra lime juice if required. Cover and leave to chill in the refrigerator.

3 To make the lime and coriander cream garnish, mix the soured cream, coriander and lime juice together in a small bowl. Spoon into the soup just before serving and sprinkle with shredded lime rind.

creamy sweetcorn soup with egg

serves four

1 tbsp vegetable oil

3 garlic cloves, crushed

1 tsp grated fresh root ginger

700 ml/1¼ pints chicken stock

375 g/13 oz canned creamed
  sweetcorn

1 tbsp Thai fish sauce

175 g/6 oz canned white
  crabmeat, drained

salt and pepper

1 egg

TO GARNISH

shredded fresh coriander

paprika

1 Heat the oil in a large, heavy-based saucepan. Add the garlic and fry for 1 minute, stirring constantly.

2 Add the ginger to the saucepan, then stir in the stock and creamed sweetcorn. Bring to the boil.

3 Stir in the fish sauce, crabmeat and salt and pepper to taste. Return the soup to the boil.

4 Beat the egg in a small bowl, then stir lightly into the soup so that it sets into long strands. Simmer gently for 30 seconds, or until just set.

5 Ladle the soup into serving bowls and serve hot, garnished with shredded coriander and paprika sprinkled over.

VARIATION

To give the soup an extra rich flavour kick for a special occasion, stir in 1 tablespoon of rice wine or dry sherry just before you ladle it into bowls.

pumpkin & coconut soup

serves six

1 kg/2 lb 4 oz pumpkin

1 tbsp groundnut oil

1 tsp yellow mustard seeds

1 garlic clove, crushed

1 large onion, chopped

1 celery stick, chopped

1 small fresh red chilli, chopped

850 ml/1½ pints chicken stock

1 tbsp dried shrimp

5 tbsp coconut cream

salt and pepper

1 Using a sharp knife, halve the pumpkin and remove the seeds. Cut away the skin and dice the flesh.

2 Heat the oil in a large, flameproof casserole. Add the mustard seeds and fry until they begin to pop. Stir in the garlic, onion, celery and chilli and stir-fry for 1–2 minutes.

3 Add the pumpkin with the stock and dried shrimp to the casserole and bring to the boil. Reduce the heat, cover and simmer for 30 minutes, or until the ingredients are very tender.

4 Transfer the mixture to a food processor or blender and process until smooth. Return to the casserole and stir in the coconut cream.

5 Season to taste with salt and pepper and serve hot.

COOK'S TIP

For an extra touch, swirl a spoonful of thick coconut milk into each bowl before serving.

25

spinach & ginger soup

serves four

2 tbsp sunflower oil

1 onion, chopped

2 garlic cloves, finely chopped

2.5-cm/1-inch piece fresh root
   ginger, finely chopped

250 g/9 oz fresh young
   spinach leaves

1 small lemon grass stalk,
   finely chopped

1 litre/1¾ pints chicken or
   vegetable stock

1 small potato, chopped

1 tbsp rice wine or dry sherry

salt and pepper

1 tsp sesame oil

VARIATION

To make a creamy-textured
spinach and coconut soup, stir in
4 tablespoons of creamed
coconut, or alternatively replace
300 ml/10 fl oz of the stock with
coconut milk. Serve the soup
with shavings of fresh coconut
sprinkled over the surface.

1 Heat the sunflower oil in a
large saucepan. Add the onion,
garlic and ginger and stir-fry gently
for 3–4 minutes, until softened but
not browned.

2 Reserve 2–3 small spinach leaves.
Add the remaining leaves and
lemon grass to the saucepan, stirring
until the spinach is wilted. Add the
stock and potato to the saucepan and
bring to the boil. Reduce the heat,
cover and simmer for 10 minutes.

3 Transfer the soup to a food
processor or blender and process
until completely smooth.

4 Return the soup to the saucepan
and add the rice wine, then
adjust the seasoning to taste with salt
and pepper. Heat until just about
to boil.

5 Finely shred the reserved spinach
leaves and sprinkle some over the
top. Drizzle with a few drops of
sesame oil and serve hot, garnished
with the remaining finely shredded
spinach leaves.

Snacks & Starters

The structure of a Thai meal is more flexible than in the West, with no starters and main courses as such; instead, snacks or appetizers  may be served in the afternoon or offered to guests before they sit down to eat a a formal meal.

Many of the recipes in this section are savoury snacks that are eaten at all times of day as well as at parties and celebrations. The Thais eat when they are hungry, and street vendors cater for this need with a huge and tempting array of wares from their stalls and bicycles – each street vendor has his own speciality of fast food, from crab cakes to spare ribs, and steamed mussels to rice soup.

tiger prawn rolls with sweet soy sauce

serves four

DIP

1 small fresh red bird's eye
　chilli, deseeded

1 tsp clear honey

4 tbsp soy sauce

PRAWN ROLLS

2 tbsp fresh coriander leaves

1 garlic clove

1½ tsp Thai red curry paste

16 wonton wrappers

1 egg white, lightly beaten

16 raw tiger prawns, peeled and
　tails left intact

sunflower oil, for deep-frying

1 To make the dip, finely chop the chilli and place in a small bowl. Add the honey and soy sauce and stir well. Reserve until required.

2 To make the prawn rolls, finely chop the coriander and garlic and place in a bowl. Add the curry paste and mix well.

3 Brush each wonton wrapper with egg white and place a small dab of the coriander mixture in the centre. Place a prawn on top.

4 Fold the wonton wrapper over, enclosing the prawn and leaving the tail exposed. Repeat with the other prawns.

5 Heat the oil for deep-frying in a large, heavy-based saucepan to 180–190°C/350–375°F, or until a cube of bread browns in 30 seconds. Deep-fry the prawns in small batches for 1–2 minutes each, or until golden brown and crisp. Drain on kitchen paper and serve with the dip.

30

fish cakes with hot peanut dip

serves four–five

350 g/12 oz skinless white fish fillet,
   such as cod or haddock
1 tbsp Thai fish sauce
2 tsp Thai red curry paste
1 tbsp lime juice
1 garlic clove, crushed
4 dried kaffir lime leaves, crumbled
1 egg white
3 tbsp chopped fresh coriander
vegetable oil, for shallow-frying
green salad leaves, to serve
PEANUT DIP
1 small fresh red chilli
1 tbsp light soy sauce
1 tbsp lime juice
1 tbsp soft light brown sugar
3 tbsp chunky peanut butter
4 tbsp coconut milk
salt and pepper
snipped fresh chives, to garnish

1 Place the fish fillet in a food processor with the fish sauce, curry paste, lime juice, garlic, lime leaves and egg white and process to a smooth paste.

2 Stir in the coriander and quickly process again until mixed. Divide the mixture into 8–10 pieces and roll into balls, then flatten to make round patties. Reserve.

3 To make the dip, halve and deseed the chilli, then chop finely. Place in a small saucepan with the remaining dip ingredients and heat gently, stirring constantly, until well blended. Adjust the seasoning to taste, if necessary, and transfer to a small bowl. Garnish with snipped chives and reserve until required.

4 Heat the oil for shallow-frying in a wide frying pan until very hot. Shallow-fry the fish cakes in batches for 3–4 minutes on each side, or until golden brown. Drain on kitchen paper and serve them hot on a bed of green salad leaves with the peanut dip.

prawn & chicken sesame toasts

makes seventy-two pieces

4 skinless, boneless chicken thighs

100 g/3½ oz cooked
   peeled prawns

1 small egg, beaten

3 spring onions, finely chopped

2 garlic cloves, crushed

2 tbsp chopped fresh coriander

1 tbsp Thai fish sauce

½ tsp pepper

¼ tsp salt

12 slices white bread,
   crusts removed

75 g/2¾ oz sesame seeds

sunflower oil, for shallow-frying

shredded spring onion curls,
   to garnish (see page 212)

1 Place the chicken and prawns in a food processor and process until very finely chopped. Add the egg, spring onions, garlic, coriander, fish sauce, pepper and salt and pulse for a few seconds to mix well. Transfer the mixture to a large bowl.

2 Spread the mixture evenly over the slices of bread, right to the edges. Sprinkle the sesame seeds over a plate and press the spread side of each slice of bread into them to coat evenly.

3 Using a sharp knife, cut the bread into small rectangles, making 6 per slice.

4 Heat a 1-cm/½-inch depth of oil in a wide frying pan until very hot. Shallow-fry the bread rectangles quickly in batches for 2–3 minutes, or until golden brown, turning them over once.

5 Drain the toasts well on kitchen paper, transfer to a serving dish and garnish with shredded spring onion curls. Serve hot.

33

tiger prawn skewers

serves four as a starter or two as a main dish

12 raw tiger prawns, in shells

3 oranges

MARINADE

2.5-cm/1-inch fresh root ginger

3 garlic cloves, crushed

2 shallots, finely chopped

1 lemon grass stalk, finely chopped

1 fresh red chilli, finely chopped

pinch of salt

1 tbsp lime juice

1 tbsp soy sauce

2 tbsp rice wine or dry sherry

TO GARNISH

fresh coriander sprigs

lime wedges

1 To make the marinade, grate the ginger and place in a food processor with the garlic, shallots, lemon grass, chilli, salt, lime juice, soy sauce and rice wine. Blend until smooth, then transfer to a shallow bowl.

2 Using a small knife or scissors, split the prawn shells down the back, but leave attached. Devein if necessary. Add to the marinade. Cover with clingfilm and leave to marinate in the refrigerator for at least 30 minutes and up to 1 hour.

3 Preheat the grill to medium. Thread each prawn onto a presoaked bamboo skewer (see Cook's Tip, page 82). Insert the skewer at the tail end and come out at the head end, until the pointed end extends at least 7.5 cm/3 inches beyond the prawn.

4 Grill for 2 minutes on each side, or until the prawns are pink and cooked through. Insert the skewers in the oranges, then transfer to a plate and garnish with the coriander sprigs and lime wedges. Serve.

open crabmeat sandwich

serves two

2 tbsp lime juice

2-cm/¾-inch piece fresh root
    ginger, grated

2-cm/¾-inch piece lemon grass,
    finely chopped

5 tbsp mayonnaise

2 large slices crusty bread

1 ripe avocado

150 g/5½ oz cooked crabmeat

pepper

fresh coriander sprigs, to garnish

lime wedges, to serve

1 Mix 1 tablespoon of the lime juice, the ginger and lemon grass together in a small bowl. Add the mayonnaise and mix well.

2 Spread 1 tablespoon of the mayonnaise smoothly over each slice of bread.

3 Halve the avocado and remove the stone. Peel and slice the flesh thinly, then arrange the slices on the bread. Sprinkle with a little of the remaining lime juice.

4 Spoon the crabmeat over the avocado, then add the remaining lime juice. Spoon over the remaining mayonnaise, season with pepper to taste, top with a coriander sprig and serve immediately with lime wedges.

COOK'S TIP

To make home-made lime-and-ginger-flavoured mayonnaise, place 2 egg yolks, 1 tablespoon lime juice and ½ teaspoon grated fresh root ginger in a blender or food processor and blend briefly. With the motor running, gradually add 300 ml/10 fl oz olive oil, drop by drop, until the mixture is thick and smooth. Season to taste with salt and pepper.

crab omelette

serves four

225 g/8 oz cooked fresh white
    crabmeat, or thawed if frozen

3 spring onions, finely chopped

1 tbsp chopped fresh coriander

1 tbsp snipped fresh chives

pinch of cayenne pepper

2 tbsp vegetable oil

2 garlic cloves, crushed

1 tsp grated fresh root ginger

1 fresh red chilli, deseeded and
    finely chopped

2 tbsp lime juice

2 fresh kaffir lime leaves, shredded

2 tsp sugar

2 tsp Thai fish sauce

3 eggs

4 tbsp coconut cream

1 tsp salt

spring onion strips, to garnish

COOK'S TIP

You can also serve this omelette
warm. After adding the crab
mixture, cook for 3–4 minutes
to allow the mixture to heat
through, then serve immediately.

1 Place the crabmeat in a bowl and check for any small pieces of shell. Add the spring onions, coriander, chives and cayenne and reserve.

2 Heat half the oil in a frying pan or preheated wok. Add the garlic, ginger and chilli and stir-fry for 30 seconds. Add the lime juice, lime leaves, sugar and fish sauce. Simmer for 3–4 minutes, or until reduced. Remove from the heat and leave to cool. Add to the crab mixture and reserve.

3 Lightly beat the eggs with the coconut cream and salt. Heat the remaining oil in a frying pan over a medium heat. Add the egg mixture and, as it sets on the base, carefully pull the edges in towards the centre, allowing the unset egg to run underneath.

4 When the egg is nearly set, spoon the crab mixture down the centre and fold the sides over. Cook for a further 1–2 minutes to finish cooking the egg, then turn the omelette out of the frying pan onto a serving dish. Leave to cool, then chill for 2–3 hours or overnight. Cut into 4 pieces, garnish with spring onion strips and serve.

steamed crab cakes

serves four

1–2 banana leaves

2 garlic cloves, crushed

1 tsp finely chopped lemon grass

½ tsp pepper

2 tbsp chopped fresh coriander

3 tbsp creamed coconut

1 tbsp lime juice

200 g/7 oz cooked crabmeat, flaked

1 tbsp Thai fish sauce

2 egg whites

1 egg yolk

8 fresh coriander leaves

sunflower oil, for deep-frying

chilli dipping sauce, to serve

1 Use the banana leaves to line 8 x 100-ml/3½-fl oz ramekin dishes or foil containers.

2 Mix the garlic, lemon grass, pepper and coriander together in a bowl. Place the creamed coconut and lime juice in a separate bowl and mash until smooth. Stir the 2 mixtures together, then add the crabmeat and fish sauce.

3 Whisk the egg whites in a clean, greasefree bowl until stiff, then lightly and evenly fold them into the crab mixture.

4 Spoon the mixture into the prepared ramekin dishes or foil containers and press down lightly. Brush the tops with egg yolk and top each with a coriander leaf.

5 Place in a steamer half-filled with boiling water, then cover with a lid and steam for 15 minutes, or until firm to the touch. Pour off the excess liquid and remove from the ramekin dishes or foil containers.

6 Heat the oil for deep-frying in a large, heavy-based saucepan to 180–190°C/350–375°F, or until a cube of bread browns in 30 seconds. Add the crab cakes and deep-fry for 1 minute, turning them over once, until golden brown. Serve hot with a chilli dipping sauce.

potato crab cakes

serves four

450 g/1 lb floury potatoes, diced

175 g/6 oz cooked white crabmeat,
    drained if canned

4 spring onions, chopped

1 tsp light soy sauce

½ tsp sesame oil

1 tsp chopped lemon grass

1 tsp lime juice

3 tbsp plain flour, plus extra
    for dusting

salt and pepper

2 tbsp vegetable oil

SAUCE

4 tbsp finely chopped cucumber

2 tbsp clear honey

1 tbsp garlic wine vinegar

½ tsp light soy sauce

1 fresh red chilli, chopped

TO GARNISH

1 fresh red chilli, sliced

cucumber slices

COOK'S TIP

Do not make the cucumber sauce
too far in advance because the
water from the cucumber will
make the sauce runny and
dilute the flavour.

1 Cook the diced potatoes in a large saucepan of boiling water for 10 minutes, or until cooked through. Drain well and mash.

2 Mix the crabmeat into the potato with the spring onions, soy sauce, sesame oil, lemon grass, lime juice and flour. Season to taste with salt and pepper.

3 Divide the potato mixture into 8 equal-sized portions and shape them into small rounds, using floured hands.

4 Heat the vegetable oil in a preheated wok or frying pan. Add the crab cakes, 4 at a time, and cook for 5–7 minutes, turning once. Keep warm and repeat with the remaining cakes.

5 Meanwhile, make the sauce. Mix the cucumber, honey, vinegar, soy sauce and chopped chilli together in a small serving bowl.

6 Garnish the crab cakes with the sliced chilli and cucumber slices and serve with the sauce.

39

mussels in spiced batter

serves four

40 large live mussels in shells

2 tbsp plain flour

2 tbsp rice flour

½ tsp salt

1 tbsp desiccated coconut

1 egg white

1 tbsp rice wine or dry sherry

2 tbsp water

1 small fresh red bird's eye chilli,
   deseeded and chopped

1 tbsp chopped fresh coriander

sunflower oil, for deep-frying

lime wedges, to serve

1 Clean the mussels thoroughly by scrubbing or scraping the shells and pulling out any beards that are attached to them. Discard any with broken shells and any that refuse to close when tapped.

2 Place the mussels in a large saucepan with just the water that clings to their shells. Cook, covered, over a high heat for 3–4 minutes, shaking the saucepan occasionally, until the mussels open. Drain well, leave to cool slightly, then remove from shells. Discard any that remain closed.

3 To make the batter, sift the plain flour, rice flour and salt into a large bowl. Add the coconut, egg white, rice wine and water and beat until well mixed and a batter forms. Stir the chilli and coriander into the batter.

4 Heat a 5-cm/2-inch depth of oil for deep-frying in a large, heavy-based saucepan to 180–190°C/ 350–375°F, or until a cube of bread browns in 30 seconds. Holding the mussels with a fork, dip them quickly into the batter, then drop into the hot oil and deep-fry for 1–2 minutes, or until crisp and golden brown.

5 Drain the mussels on kitchen paper and serve hot with lime wedges to squeeze over.

COOK'S TIP

If you reserve the mussel shells, the cooked mussels can be replaced in them to serve.

40

fragrant mussels

**serves four as a starter
or two as a main dish**

1 kg/2 lb 4 oz live mussels in shells

2 tbsp water

1 lemon grass stalk, bruised

2 garlic cloves, crushed

3 fresh or dried kaffir lime leaves

200 ml/7 fl oz coconut cream

2 tbsp chopped fresh coriander

salt and pepper

warm crusty bread, to serve

1 Clean the mussels by scrubbing or scraping the shells and pulling out any beards that are attached. Discard any with broken shells and any that refuse to close when tapped.

2 Chop the lime leaves and place in a large saucepan with the water, lemon grass and garlic. Heat until boiling. Add the mussels, cover and cook for 3–4 minutes, or until they have opened. Discard any mussels that remain closed. Transfer to a serving dish, cover and place in a low oven.

3 Boil the cooking liquid hard until reduced by half, then stir in the coconut cream. Boil to reduce and thicken slightly. Stir in the coriander and add salt and pepper to taste.

4 Pour over the mussels and serve with warm crusty bread.

41

steamed mussels with lemon grass & basil

serves four as a starter or two as a main dish

1 kg/2 lb 4 oz live mussels in shells

2 shallots, finely chopped

1 lemon grass stalk, finely sliced

1 garlic clove, finely chopped

3 tbsp rice wine or dry sherry

2 tbsp lime juice

1 tbsp Thai fish sauce

4 tbsp chopped fresh basil

salt and pepper

25 g/1 oz butter

fresh basil leaves, to garnish

crusty bread, to serve

COOK'S TIP

Fresh clams in shells are also very good when cooked by this method.

1 Clean the mussels thoroughly by scrubbing or scraping the shells and pulling out any beards that are attached to them. Discard any with broken shells or any that refuse to close when tapped.

2 Place the shallots, lemon grass, garlic, rice wine, lime juice and fish sauce in a large, heavy-based saucepan and place over a high heat.

3 Add the mussels, then cover and steam for 3–4 minutes, shaking the saucepan occasionally, until the mussels have opened.

4 Discard any mussels that remain closed, then stir in the chopped basil and season to taste with salt and pepper.

5 Scoop out the mussels with a slotted spoon and divide between 4 deep bowls. Quickly whisk the butter into the pan juices, then pour the juices over the mussels.

6 Garnish each bowl with fresh basil leaves and serve with plenty of crusty bread to mop up the juices.

42

roasted spare ribs with honey & soy

serves four

1 kg/2 lb 4 oz Chinese-style
    spare ribs

½ lemon

½ small orange

2.5-cm/1-inch piece fresh
    root ginger

2 garlic cloves

1 small onion, chopped

2 tbsp soy sauce

2 tbsp rice wine or dry sherry

½ tsp Thai seven-spice powder

2 tbsp clear honey

1 tbsp sesame oil

lemon twists, to garnish

orange wedges, to serve

1 Preheat the oven to 180°C/ 350°F/Gas Mark 4. Place the spare ribs in a wide roasting tin, cover loosely with foil and cook for 30 minutes.

2 Meanwhile, remove any pips from the lemon and orange and place them in a food processor with the ginger, garlic, onion, soy sauce, rice wine, seven-spice powder, honey and oil. Process until smooth.

3 Increase the oven temperature to 200°C/400°F/Gas Mark 6. Pour off any fat from the spare ribs, then spoon the puréed mixture over the spare ribs and toss to coat evenly.

4 Return the ribs to the oven and roast for 40 minutes, turning and basting them occasionally, until golden brown. Garnish with lemon twists and serve hot with orange wedges.

crispy pork & peanut baskets

serves four

2 sheets filo pastry, about 42 x
   28 cm/16½ x 11 inches each
1 tbsp vegetable oil, plus extra
   for brushing
1 garlic clove, crushed
125 g/4½ oz minced pork
1 tsp Thai red curry paste
2 spring onions, finely chopped
3 tbsp crunchy peanut butter
1 tbsp light soy sauce
1 tbsp chopped fresh coriander
salt and pepper
fresh coriander sprigs, to garnish

1 Preheat the oven to 200°C/
400°F/Gas Mark 6. Cut each
sheet of filo pastry into 24 x 7-cm/
2¾-inch squares, to make a total of
48 squares. Brush each square lightly
with oil and arrange the squares in
stacks of 4 in 12 small patty tins,
pointing outwards. Press the pastry
down into the patty tins.

2 Bake the pastry cases in the
preheated oven for 6–8 minutes,
or until golden brown.

3 Meanwhile, heat 1 tablespoon of
oil in a heavy-based frying pan.
Add the garlic and fry for 30 seconds,
then stir in the pork and stir-fry over a
high heat for 4–5 minutes, or until the
meat is golden brown.

4 Add the curry paste and spring
onions and continue to stir-fry for
a further 1 minute, then stir in the
peanut butter, soy sauce and coriander.
Season to taste with salt and pepper.

5 Spoon the pork mixture into
the filo baskets, garnish with
coriander sprigs and serve hot.

COOK'S TIP
When using filo pastry,
remember that it dries out very
quickly and becomes brittle and
difficult to handle. Work quickly
and keep any sheets of pastry
you're not using covered with
clingfilm and a dampened cloth.

lemon grass chicken skewers

serves four

2 long or 4 short lemon grass stalks

2 large skinless, boneless chicken
  breasts, about 400 g/14 oz
  in total

1 small egg white

1 carrot, finely grated

1 small fresh red chilli, deseeded
  and chopped

2 tbsp snipped fresh garlic chives

2 tbsp chopped fresh coriander

salt and pepper

1 tbsp sunflower oil

TO GARNISH

fresh coriander sprigs

lime slices

mixed salad leaves, to serve

1 If the lemon grass stalks are long, cut them in half across the centre to make 4 short lengths. Cut each stalk in half lengthways, so that you have 8 sticks.

2 Roughly chop the chicken pieces and place them in a food processor with the egg white. Process to a smooth paste, then add the carrot, chilli, chives, coriander, and salt and pepper to taste. Process for a few seconds to mix well. Transfer to a large bowl, cover and chill in the refrigerator for 15 minutes.

3 Preheat the grill to medium. Divide the mixture into 8 equal-sized portions and use your hands to shape the mixture around the lemon grass 'skewers'.

VARIATION

If you can't find whole lemon grass stalks, use presoaked wooden skewers instead (see Cook's Tip, page 82), and add ½ teaspoon ground lemon grass to the mixture with the other flavourings.

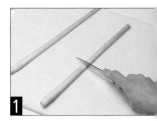

4 Brush the skewers with oil and cook under the hot grill for 4–6 minutes, turning them occasionally, until golden brown and thoroughly cooked. Alternatively, barbecue over medium–hot coals.

5 Transfer to serving plates, garnish with coriander sprigs and lime slices and serve hot with salad leaves.

steamed wonton bundles

serves four

125 g/4½ oz minced pork

1 tbsp dried shrimp, finely chopped

1 fresh green chilli, finely chopped

2 shallots, finely chopped

1 tsp cornflour

1 small egg, beaten

2 tsp dark soy sauce

2 tsp rice wine or dry sherry

salt and pepper

12 wonton wrappers

1 tsp sesame oil

chilli dipping sauce, to serve

1 Mix the pork, dried shrimp, chilli and shallots together in a bowl. Blend the cornflour with half the egg and stir into the pork mixture with the soy sauce and rice wine. Season to taste with salt and pepper.

2 Arrange the wonton wrappers flat on a clean work surface and place 1 tablespoon of the pork mixture onto the centre of each wrapper.

3 Brush the wrappers with the remaining egg and carefully pull up the edges, pinching together lightly at the top and leaving a small gap so that the filling can just be seen.

4 Place enough water in the base of a steamer and bring to the boil. Brush the inside of the top part of the steamer with sesame oil.

5 Arrange the wontons in the top, cover and steam for 15–20 minutes. Serve hot with a chilli dipping sauce.

stuffed chicken wings

serves four

8 chicken wings

3 tbsp dried shrimp

3 tbsp hot water

200 g/7 oz minced pork

1 garlic clove, crushed

1 tbsp Thai fish sauce

$\frac{1}{2}$ tsp salt

$\frac{1}{2}$ tsp pepper

2 spring onions, finely chopped

$\frac{1}{4}$ tsp ground turmeric

1 small egg, beaten

2 tbsp rice flour

sunflower oil, for deep-frying

fresh red chillies, to garnish

TO SERVE

cucumber slices

chilli dipping sauce

1 Using a small, sharp knife, cut around the end of the bone at the cut end of each wing, then loosen the flesh away from around the bone, scraping it downwards with the knife and pulling back the skin as you go. When you reach the next joint, grasp the end of the bone and twist sharply to break it at the joint. Remove the bone and turn back the flesh.

2 Continue to scrape the meat away down the length of the next long bone, exposing the joint. Twist to break the bone at the joint and remove, leaving just the wing tip in place.

3 Meanwhile, soak the dried shrimp in the hot water for 10–15 minutes. Drain, then chop. Place the pork, shrimp, garlic, fish sauce, salt and pepper into a food processor and process to a smooth paste. Transfer to a bowl and add the spring onions. Stir well. Use the mixture to stuff the chicken wings, pressing it down inside with your finger.

4 Beat the turmeric into the beaten egg and reserve until required. Dip each wing into the rice flour, shaking off the excess.

5 Heat a 5-cm/2-inch depth of oil in a large, heavy-based saucepan to 180–190°C/350–375°F, or until a cube of bread browns in 30 seconds. Dip the floured chicken wings quickly into the beaten egg, then drop carefully into the hot oil and deep-fry in small batches for 8–10 minutes, turning them over once. Drain the chicken wings on kitchen paper. Garnish with chillies and serve with cucumber slices and a chilli dipping sauce.

48

chicken satay

serves eight

900 g/2 lb chicken breasts,
    cut into 5-mm/¼-inch thick,
    2.5-cm/1-inch wide strips
MARINADE
1 lemon grass stalk (tender inner
    part only)
2 tbsp vegetable oil
2 tbsp soy sauce
2 tsp tamarind paste
2 garlic cloves, crushed
1 tsp ground cumin
1 tsp ground coriander
1 tbsp lime juice
1 tsp soft light brown sugar
PEANUT SAUCE
2 tbsp smooth peanut butter
200 ml/7 fl oz coconut cream
2 tsp Thai red curry paste
1 tbsp fish sauce
1 tbsp soft light brown sugar

1 Thread the chicken onto presoaked bamboo skewers (see Cook's Tip, page 82).

2 To make the marinade, chop the lemon grass and place in a food processor with the oil, soy sauce, tamarind paste, garlic, cumin, coriander, lime juice and sugar. Process to a paste. Transfer to a bowl.

3 Add the chicken to the marinade and toss to coat. Cover with clingfilm and leave to marinate in the refrigerator for at least 1 hour.

4 Preheat the grill to medium. Place the peanut butter, coconut cream, red curry paste, fish sauce and sugar in a saucepan. Heat gently, stirring constantly, to form a smooth sauce.

5 Cook the chicken under the hot grill for 3–5 minutes on each side, or until the chicken is cooked through. Alternatively, barbecue over medium–hot coals. Reheat the sauce, adding a little hot water if necessary, and serve with the chicken satays.

hot chilli relish with crudités

serves four

RELISH

6 garlic cloves

8–10 large fresh red chillies,
 deseeded and finely chopped

125 ml/4 fl oz water

½ tsp salt

2 tsp sugar

juice of 1 lime

1 tbsp Thai fish sauce

1 tbsp vegetable oil

CRUDITES

carrot sticks

radishes

cucumber batons

baby corn cobs

1 Finely chop the garlic and place in a preheated wok with the remaining relish ingredients. Bring to the boil, cover and simmer for 10 minutes.

2 Transfer the mixture to a food processor and blend until smooth.

3 Prepare the Crudités. Transfer the relish to a bowl and serve with the crudités.

51

sticky ginger chicken wings

serves four

2 garlic cloves, roughly chopped

1 piece stem ginger in syrup,
  roughly chopped

1 tsp coriander seeds

2 tbsp stem ginger syrup

2 tbsp dark soy sauce

1 tbsp lime juice

1 tsp sesame oil

12 chicken wings

TO GARNISH

lime wedges

fresh coriander leaves

1 Place the garlic, stem ginger and coriander seeds in a mortar and, using a pestle, crush to a paste, gradually working in the ginger syrup, soy sauce, lime juice and sesame oil.

2 Tuck the pointed tip of each chicken wing underneath the thicker end of the wing to make a neat triangular shape. Place in a large bowl.

3 Add the garlic and ginger paste to the bowl and toss the chicken wings in the mixture to coat evenly. Cover with clingfilm and leave to marinate in the refrigerator for several hours or overnight.

4 Preheat the grill to medium. Arrange the chicken wings in a single layer on a foil-lined grill pan and cook under the hot grill for 12–15 minutes, turning them occasionally, until golden brown and thoroughly cooked.

5 Alternatively, cook on a lightly oiled barbecue grill over medium–hot coals. Transfer to individual plates, garnish with lime wedges and coriander leaves, then serve immediately.

52

chicken fried in banana leaves

serves four–six

1 garlic clove, chopped

1 tsp finely chopped fresh
   root ginger

¼ tsp pepper

2 fresh coriander sprigs

1 tbsp Thai fish sauce

1 tbsp whisky

3 skinless, boneless chicken breasts

2–3 banana leaves, cut into 7.5-cm/
   3-inch squares

sunflower oil, for shallow-frying

chilli dipping sauce, to serve

COOK'S TIP

To make a sweet chilli dipping
sauce to serve with the chicken
pieces, mix equal amounts of
chilli sauce and tomato ketchup
together, then stir in a dash of
rice wine to taste.

1 Place the garlic, ginger, pepper,
coriander sprigs, fish sauce and
whisky in a mortar and, using a pestle,
grind to a smooth paste.

2 Cut the chicken into 2.5-cm/
1-inch chunks and toss in the
paste to coat evenly. Cover and
marinate in the refrigerator for 1 hour.

3 Place a piece of chicken on a
square of banana leaf and wrap it
up like a parcel to enclose the chicken
completely. Secure with wooden
cocktail sticks or tie with a piece
of string.

4 Heat a 3-mm/⅛-inch depth of
oil in a large, heavy-based frying
pan until hot.

5 Shallow-fry the parcels for
8–10 minutes, turning them over
occasionally, until golden brown and
the chicken is thoroughly cooked.
Serve with a chilli dipping sauce.

53

chicken balls with dipping sauce

serves four–six

2 large skinless, boneless chicken
   breasts, coarsely chopped

3 tbsp vegetable oil

2 shallots, finely chopped

½ celery stick, finely chopped

1 garlic clove, crushed

2 tbsp light soy sauce

1 small egg, lightly beaten

salt and pepper

1 bunch of spring onions

spring onion tassels, to garnish
   (see Cook's Tip, page 100)

DIPPING SAUCE

3 tbsp dark soy sauce

1 tbsp rice wine or dry sherry

1 tsp sesame seeds

1 Cut the chicken into 2-cm/¾-inch pieces. Heat half of the oil in a large frying pan. Add the chicken and stir-fry over a high heat for 2–3 minutes, until golden. Remove the chicken with a slotted spoon and reserve until required.

2 Add the shallots, celery and garlic to the frying pan and stir-fry for 1–2 minutes, or until softened but not browned.

3 Place the reserved chicken, shallots, celery and garlic in a food processor and process until finely minced. Add 1 tablespoon of the light soy sauce, just enough egg to make a fairly firm mixture and salt and pepper to taste.

4 Trim the spring onions and cut into 5-cm/2-inch lengths. Reserve until required. Make the dipping sauce by mixing the dark soy sauce, rice wine and sesame seeds together in a small bowl. Reserve.

5 Form the chicken mixture into 16–18 walnut-sized balls between the palms of your hands. Heat the remaining oil in the frying pan and stir-fry the balls in small batches for 4–5 minutes, or until golden brown. As each batch is cooked, drain on kitchen paper and keep hot.

6 Stir-fry the reserved spring onions for 1–2 minutes, or until they begin to soften, then stir in the remaining light soy sauce. Serve with the chicken balls and dipping sauce, garnished with spring onion tassels.

54

spring rolls

makes thirty

1 tbsp vegetable oil

250 g/9 oz lean minced pork

1 garlic clove, crushed

1 fresh red chilli, deseeded and
finely chopped

115 g/4 oz cooked peeled prawns

2 spring onions, finely chopped

2.5-cm/1-inch piece fresh root
ginger, finely grated

2 tbsp chopped fresh coriander

2 tsp Thai fish sauce

30 spring roll wrappers

sunflower oil, for deep-frying

sweet chilli dipping sauce, to serve

1 Heat the vegetable oil in a frying pan. Add the pork, garlic and chilli. Cook, stirring, until the pork is browned.

2 Chop the prawns, then add to the frying pan with the spring onions, ginger, coriander and fish sauce. Cook, stirring, until heated through. Remove the frying pan from the heat and leave to cool.

3 Prepare the spring roll wrappers according to the packet instructions.

4 Place a spoonful of the pork mixture down the centre of each spring roll wrapper, leaving a space at the top and bottom and down the side. Brush the edges with water. Fold the top and bottom over and then fold in the sides to form a sealed roll.

5 Just before serving, heat the oil for deep-frying in a large saucepan or wok until nearly smoking. Deep-fry the rolls in batches for 2–3 minutes, or until golden brown. Drain on kitchen paper and keep warm while frying the remainder. Serve with a sweet chilli dipping sauce.

55

stuffed eggs with pork & crabmeat

serves four

4 large eggs

100 g/3½ oz minced pork

175 g/6 oz canned white
    crabmeat, drained

1 garlic clove, crushed

1 tsp Thai fish sauce

½ tsp ground lemon grass

1 tbsp chopped fresh coriander

1 tbsp desiccated coconut

salt and pepper

100 g/3½ oz plain flour

about 150 ml/5 fl oz coconut milk

sunflower oil, for deep-frying

cucumber flowers, to garnish

green salad, to serve

1 Place the eggs in a saucepan of simmering water and bring to the boil, then leave to simmer for 10 minutes. Drain the eggs, crack the shells and cool under cold running water. Peel off the shells.

2 Cut the eggs lengthways down the centre and scoop out the yolks. Place the yolks in a bowl with the pork, crabmeat, garlic, fish sauce, lemon grass, coriander and coconut. Season to taste with salt and pepper and mix well.

3 Divide the mixture into 8 equal-sized portions, then fill each of the egg whites with the mixture, pressing together with your hands to form the shape of a whole egg.

4 Whisk the flour and enough coconut milk together to form a thick batter. Season to taste.

5 Heat a 5-cm/2-inch depth of oil in a large, heavy-based saucepan to 180–190°C/350–375°F, or until a cube of bread browns in 30 seconds. Dip each egg into the coconut batter, then shake off the excess.

6 Deep-fry the eggs in batches for 5 minutes, turning occasionally, until golden brown. Remove with a slotted spoon and drain on kitchen paper. Transfer to plates, garnish with cucumber flowers and serve with a green salad.

pork appetizer in lettuce cups

serves six

2 fresh red chillies

4 garlic cloves, finely chopped

1 tbsp chopped coriander root

1 tbsp grated fresh root ginger

3 tbsp vegetable oil

1 tbsp hot water

500 g/1 lb 2 oz lean minced pork

2 fresh kaffir lime leaves,
    finely shredded

2 tbsp Thai fish sauce

1 tsp soft light brown sugar

2 tbsp roughly chopped fresh
    coriander

12 leaves Cos lettuce, or similar firm
    lettuce leaves (see page 194)

TO GARNISH

fresh coriander leaves

thin strips of fresh red chilli

1 Deseed and finely chop the chillies, then place in a blender or food processor with the garlic, coriander root, ginger, oil and water. Process until smooth.

2 Transfer to a preheated wok or large frying pan.

3 Stir-fry the paste for 4 minutes over a medium heat, then increase the heat and add the pork. Stir-fry for a further 3 minutes, or until coloured.

4 Add the lime leaves, fish sauce, sugar and chopped coriander. Continue to stir-fry until the pork is dry.

5 Arrange the pork in lettuce cups, garnish with coriander leaves and strips of chilli and serve.

57

pork-stuffed omelette

serves four

2 garlic cloves, chopped

4 black peppercorns

4 fresh coriander sprigs

2 tbsp vegetable oil

200 g/7 oz minced pork

2 spring onions, chopped

1 large firm tomato, chopped

6 large eggs

1 tbsp Thai fish sauce

$\frac{1}{4}$ tsp ground turmeric

mixed salad leaves, tossed, to serve

1 Place the garlic, peppercorns and coriander in a mortar and, using a pestle, grind to a smooth paste.

2 Heat 1 tablespoon of the oil in a large frying pan. Add the paste and stir-fry for 1–2 minutes, or until it just changes colour.

3 Stir in the pork and stir-fry until it is lightly browned. Add the spring onions and tomato, and stir-fry for a further 1 minute, then remove the frying pan from the heat.

4 Heat the remaining oil in a small, heavy-based frying pan. Beat the eggs with the fish sauce and turmeric, then pour one-quarter of the egg mixture into the frying pan. As the mixture begins to set, stir lightly to ensure that all the liquid egg is set.

5 Spoon one-quarter of the pork mixture down the centre of the omelette, then fold the sides inwards towards the centre, enclosing the filling. Transfer to a heatproof plate and keep warm. Make 3 more omelettes with the remaining egg and fill with the remaining pork mixture.

6 Slide the omelettes onto serving plates and serve with salad.

58

vegetarian spring rolls

serves four

25 g/1 oz fine cellophane noodles

2 tbsp groundnut oil, plus extra for deep-frying

2 garlic cloves, crushed

½ tsp grated fresh root ginger

55 g/2 oz oyster mushrooms, thinly sliced

2 spring onions, finely chopped

50 g/1¾ oz beansprouts

1 small carrot, finely shredded

½ tsp sesame oil

1 tbsp light soy sauce

1 tbsp rice wine or dry sherry

¼ tsp pepper

1 tbsp chopped fresh coriander

1 tbsp chopped fresh mint

24 spring roll wrappers

½ tsp cornflour

1 fresh mint sprig, to garnish

chilli dipping sauce, to serve

1 Place the noodles in a heatproof bowl, pour over enough boiling water to cover and leave to stand for 4 minutes. Drain, rinse in cold water, then drain again. Use a sharp knife to cut into 5-cm/2-inch lengths.

2 Heat the groundnut oil in a preheated wok or frying pan. Add the garlic, ginger, mushrooms, spring onions, beansprouts and carrot. Stir-fry for 1 minute, or until soft.

3 Stir in the sesame oil, soy sauce, rice wine, pepper, coriander and mint, then remove the wok from the heat. Stir in the noodles.

4 Arrange the spring roll wrappers on a work surface, pointing diagonally. Mix the cornflour with a little water and use to brush the edges of a wrapper. Spoon some filling onto the pointed side of the same wrapper.

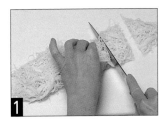

5 Roll the point of the wrapper over the filling, then fold the side points inwards over the filling. Continue to roll up the wrapper away from you, moistening the tip with more cornflour mixture to secure the roll. Make up all the spring rolls in the same way.

6 Heat the oil for deep-frying in a wok or deep frying pan to 180–190°C/350–375°F, or until a cube of bread browns in 30 seconds. Deep-fry the rolls in batches for 2–3 minutes each, until golden brown and crisp. Drain and transfer to a plate. Garnish with a mint sprig and serve with a chilli dipping sauce.

59

tuna & tomato salad with ginger dressing

serves four

50 g/1¾ oz Chinese
   leaves, shredded
3 tbsp rice wine or dry sherry
2 tbsp Thai fish sauce
1 tbsp finely shredded fresh
   root ginger
1 garlic clove, finely chopped
½ small fresh red bird's eye chilli,
   finely chopped
2 tsp soft light brown sugar
2 tbsp lime juice
400 g/14 oz fresh tuna steak
sunflower oil, for brushing
125 g/4½ oz cherry tomatoes
fresh mint leaves and mint sprigs,
   roughly chopped, to garnish

COOK'S TIP
The dressing can be made in
advance and spooned over the
dish just before serving.

1 Place a small pile of shredded
Chinese leaves on a large serving
plate. Place the rice wine, fish sauce,
ginger, garlic, chilli, sugar and
1 tablespoon of lime juice in a screw-
top jar and shake well to combine.

2 Using a sharp knife, cut the tuna
into strips of an even thickness.
Sprinkle with the remaining lime juice.

3 Brush a wide frying pan or ridged
grill pan with oil and heat until
very hot. Arrange the tuna strips in the
frying pan and cook until just firm and
light golden, turning them over once.
Remove the tuna from the frying pan
and reserve.

4 Add the tomatoes to the frying
pan and cook over a high heat
until lightly browned. Spoon the tuna
and tomatoes over the Chinese leaves,
then spoon over the dressing. Garnish
with fresh mint and serve warm.

60

sweet & sour seafood salad

serves six

18 live mussels in shells

6 large scallops, shelled

200 g/7 oz baby squid, cleaned

2 shallots, finely chopped

6 raw tiger prawns, peeled
and deveined

¼ cucumber

1 carrot

¼ head Chinese leaves, shredded

DRESSING

4 tbsp lime juice

2 garlic cloves, finely chopped

2 tbsp Thai fish sauce

1 tsp sesame oil

1 tbsp soft light brown sugar

2 tbsp chopped fresh mint

½ tsp pepper

salt

1 Clean the mussels thoroughly by scrubbing or scraping the shells and pulling out any beards that are attached to them. Discard any with broken shells and any that refuse to close when tapped. Place the mussels in a large saucepan with just the water that clings to their shells and cook, covered, for 3–4 minutes, shaking the pan occasionally, until they have opened. Remove the mussels with a slotted spoon, reserving the liquid in the saucepan. Discard any that remain closed.

2 Using a sharp knife, separate the corals from the scallops, then cut the white parts in half horizontally. Cut the tentacles from the squid and slice the body cavities into rings.

3 Add the shallots to the liquid in the saucepan and simmer over a high heat until the liquid is reduced to 3 tablespoons. Add the scallops, squid and tiger prawns and stir for 2–3 minutes, or until cooked. Remove the saucepan from the heat and transfer the mixture to a wide bowl. Add the mussels.

4 Cut the cucumber and carrot in half lengthways, then slice thinly on a diagonal angle to make long, pointed slices. Toss with the Chinese leaves. To make the dressing, place all the ingredients in a screw-top jar and shake well until evenly combined. Season to taste with salt.

5 Add the vegetables to the seafood in the bowl and toss together. Spoon the dressing over and serve immediately.

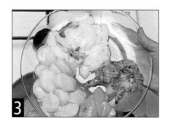

62

Fish & Seafood

The Thais are primarily a fish-eating nation, with meat often being reserved for special celebrations. The waterways of Thailand are teeming with many types of fish – even in the channels between the paddy fields – and the warm seas bring an abundance of fish and shellfish.

Even in the heart of Bangkok city, the markets are packed with fresh fish and seafood of all kinds. In coastal towns, rows of thatch-roofed beach kiosks sell every type of fresh seafood from the warm Gulf waters – from barbecued or sautéed fish with ginger to prawns in coconut milk and coriander – to locals and visitors alike.

steamed yellow fish fillets

serves four

500 g/1 lb 2 oz firm fish fillets, such
    as red snapper, sole or monkfish

1 dried red bird's eye chilli

1 small onion, chopped

3 garlic cloves, chopped

2 fresh coriander sprigs

1 tsp coriander seeds

$\frac{1}{2}$ tsp ground turmeric

$\frac{1}{2}$ tsp pepper

1 tbsp Thai fish sauce

2 tbsp coconut milk

1 small egg, beaten

2 tbsp rice flour

fresh red and green chilli strips,
    to garnish

stir-fried vegetables, to serve

1 Using a sharp knife, remove any skin from the fish and cut the fillets diagonally into 2-cm/¾-inch wide strips.

2 Place the dried chilli, onion, garlic, coriander and coriander seeds in a mortar and, using a pestle, grind to a smooth paste.

3 Transfer the paste to a bowl and add the turmeric, pepper, fish sauce, coconut milk and beaten egg, stirring to mix evenly. Spread the rice flour out on a large plate. Dip the fish strips into the paste mixture, then into the rice flour to coat lightly.

4 Bring the water in the base of a steamer to the boil, then arrange the fish strips in the top of the steamer. Cover and steam for 12–15 minutes, or until the fish is just firm.

5 Garnish the fish with the chilli strips and serve immediately with stir-fried vegetables.

fish curry

serves four

4 shallots, roughly chopped

5-cm/2-inch piece fresh root ginger,
peeled and finely sliced

5-cm/2-inch piece lemon grass,
outer leaves discarded

5-cm/2-inch piece fresh galangal,
finely chopped

3 fresh red chillies, deseeded and
roughly chopped

1 tbsp ground almonds

½ tsp ground turmeric

½ tsp salt

400 ml/14 fl oz coconut cream

4 fish steaks, such as cod, turbot
or halibut

salad, to serve

TO GARNISH

1 fresh red chilli, cut into thin strips

2 tbsp toasted flaked almonds

1 Roughly chop the shallots and place in a blender or food processor with the ginger, lemon grass, galangal, chillies, almonds, turmeric and salt. Add 6 tablespoons of the coconut cream and process to a smooth paste.

2 Pour the paste into a large saucepan. Bring to the boil and cook, stirring constantly, for 4 minutes. Add the remaining coconut cream and return to the boil.

3 Place the fish steaks in the saucepan and leave to simmer for 10 minutes, turning once, until the fish is cooked and flakes easily when tested with a fork. If the sauce is too thin, transfer the fish to a warmed serving dish and boil the sauce to reduce to the desired consistency. Garnish with chilli strips and toasted slivered almonds and serve with a salad of your choice.

baked fish with pepper, chillies & basil

serves four

handful of fresh basil leaves

750 g/1 lb 10 oz whole red
  snapper, sea bass or
  John Dory, cleaned

2 tbsp groundnut oil

2 tbsp Thai fish sauce

2 garlic cloves, crushed

1 tsp finely grated fresh root ginger
  or galangal

2 large fresh red chillies,
  diagonally sliced

1 yellow pepper, deseeded
  and diced

1 tbsp palm sugar

1 tbsp rice vinegar or white
  wine vinegar

2 tbsp water or fish stock

2 tomatoes, deseeded and sliced
  into thin wedges

mixed salad, to serve

COOK'S TIP
Almost any whole fish can be
cooked by this method, but
snapper, sea bass or John Dory
are particularly good with the
Thai flavours.

1 Preheat the oven to 190°C/375°F/
Gas Mark 5. Reserve a few basil
leaves for the garnish and tuck the rest
inside the body cavity of the fish.

2 Heat 1 tablespoon of the oil in
a wide frying pan. Add the fish
and fry quickly to brown, turning once.
Place the fish on a large piece of foil
in a roasting tin and spoon over the
fish sauce. Wrap the foil over the fish
loosely and bake in the preheated
oven for 25–30 minutes, or until just
cooked through.

3 Meanwhile, heat the remaining
oil in a clean frying pan. Add the
garlic, ginger and chillies and fry for
30 seconds. Add the pepper and stir-
fry for a further 2–3 minutes to soften.

4 Stir in the sugar, rice vinegar and
water, then add the tomatoes and
bring to the boil. Remove the frying
pan from the heat.

5 Remove the fish from the oven
and transfer to a warmed serving
plate. Add the fish juices to the frying
pan, then spoon the sauce over the fish.
Sprinkle with the reserved basil leaves
and serve immediately with a salad.

68

curried mussel soup

serves four

1 tsp coriander seeds

1 tsp cumin seeds

900 g/2 lb live mussels in shells

100 ml/3 fl oz white wine

50 g/1¾ oz butter

1 onion, finely chopped

1 garlic clove, finely chopped

1 tsp freshly grated root ginger

1 tsp ground turmeric

pinch of cayenne pepper

600 ml/1 pint fish stock

4 tbsp double cream

25 g/1 oz plain flour

2 tbsp chopped fresh coriander, to garnish

1 Fry the coriander and cumin seeds in a dry frying pan until they begin to smell aromatic and start to pop. Transfer to a mortar and, using a pestle, grind to a powder. Reserve.

2 Clean the mussels by scrubbing or scraping the shells and pulling out any beards that are attached to them. Discard any with broken shells or any that refuse to close when tapped. Place the mussels in a large saucepan with the wine and cook, covered, over a high heat for 3–4 minutes, shaking the saucepan occasionally, until the mussels have opened. Discard any mussels that remain closed. Drain, reserving the cooking liquid, and leave the mussels until cool enough to handle. Remove two-thirds of the mussels from their shells and set them all aside. Pour the mussel cooking liquid through a sieve and reserve.

3 Heat half the butter in a large saucepan. Add the onion and fry gently for 4–5 minutes, until softened, but not coloured. Add the garlic and ginger and cook for a further 1 minute before adding the roasted and ground spices, the turmeric and cayenne. Fry for 1 minute before adding the stock, reserved mussel cooking liquid and cream. Simmer for 10 minutes.

4 Cream the remaining butter and flour together to a thick paste. Add the paste to the simmering soup and stir until dissolved and the soup has thickened slightly. Add the mussels and heat gently for 2 minutes. Garnish with coriander and serve.

fish cakes with sweet & sour dip

serves four

450 g/1 lb firm white fish, skinned
  and roughly chopped

1 tbsp Thai fish sauce

1 tbsp Thai red curry paste

1 fresh kaffir lime leaf, shredded

2 tbsp chopped fresh coriander

1 egg

1 tsp brown sugar

large pinch of salt

40 g/1½ oz green beans, thinly
  sliced crossways

vegetable oil, for shallow-frying

SWEET & SOUR DIP

4 tbsp sugar

1 tbsp cold water

3 tbsp white rice vinegar

2 small fresh chillies, finely chopped

1 tbsp Thai fish sauce

TO GARNISH

spring onion tassels (see page 100)

fresh red chilli flowers
  (see page 160)

COOK'S TIP

It isn't necessary to use the
most expensive cut of white fish
in this recipe because the other
flavours are very strong.

1 To make the fish cakes, place the fish, fish sauce, curry paste, lime leaf, coriander, egg, sugar and salt into a food processor and process until smooth. Scrape into a bowl and stir in the green beans. Reserve.

2 To make the dipping sauce, place the sugar, water and rice vinegar in a small saucepan and heat gently until the sugar has dissolved. Bring to the boil, then reduce the heat and simmer for 2 minutes. Remove the saucepan from the heat and stir in the chillies and fish sauce. Leave to cool until required.

3 Heat a frying pan with enough oil to cover the base generously. Divide the fish mixture into 16 balls. Flatten the balls into patties and fry in the oil for 1–2 minutes on each side until golden. Drain on kitchen paper. Garnish with spring onion tassels and chilli flowers and serve with the dip.

71

whole fried fish with soy & ginger

serves four–six

6 dried shiitake mushrooms

3 tbsp rice vinegar

2 tbsp soft light brown sugar

3 tbsp dark soy sauce

7.5-cm/3-inch piece fresh root
   ginger, finely chopped

4 spring onions, diagonally sliced

2 tsp cornflour

2 tbsp lime juice

1 sea bass, about 1 kg/
   2 lb 4 oz, cleaned

salt and pepper

4 tbsp plain flour

sunflower oil, for frying

1 radish, sliced but left whole,
   to garnish

TO SERVE

shredded Chinese leaves

radish slices

COOK'S TIP

Buy a very fresh whole fish on
the day you plan to cook it, and
ask your fishmonger to clean it,
preferably leaving the head on.

1 Place the dried mushrooms in a
bowl, cover with hot water and
leave to soak for 10 minutes. Drain
well, reserving 100 ml/3½ fl oz of the
liquid. Using a sharp knife, cut the
mushrooms into thin slices.

2 Mix the reserved mushroom
liquid with the rice vinegar, sugar
and soy sauce. Place in a saucepan
with the mushrooms. Bring to the boil,
then reduce the heat and simmer for
3–4 minutes.

3 Add the ginger and spring onions
and simmer for 1 minute. Blend
the cornflour and lime juice together,
add to the saucepan and stir for
1–2 minutes, until the sauce thickens
and clears. Reserve until required.

4 Season the fish inside and out,
then dust lightly with flour,
carefully shaking off the excess.

5 Heat a 2.5-cm/1-inch depth of oil in
a wide frying pan to 180–190°C/
350–375°F, or until a cube of bread
browns in 30 seconds. Carefully lower
the fish into the oil and fry on one side
for 3–4 minutes, or until golden.
Use 2 metal spatulas to turn the fish
and fry on the other side for a further
3–4 minutes, until golden brown.

6 Lift the fish out of the frying pan,
draining off the excess oil,
and place on a serving plate. Heat the
reserved sauce until boiling, then spoon
it over the fish. Serve immediately,
surrounded by shredded Chinese
leaves with radish slices, and
garnished with the sliced radish.

72

baked cod with a curry crust

serves four

½ tsp sesame oil

4 cod fillet pieces, about
  150 g/5½ oz each

85 g/3 oz fresh white breadcrumbs

2 tbsp blanched almonds, chopped

2 tsp Thai green curry paste

finely grated rind of ½ lime, plus
  extra to garnish

salt and pepper

lime slices, to garnish

TO SERVE

boiled new potatoes

mixed salad leaves

1 Preheat the oven to 200°C/400°F/ Gas Mark 6. Brush the oil over the base of a wide, shallow, ovenproof dish or tin, then arrange the cod pieces in a single layer.

2 Mix the breadcrumbs, almonds, curry paste and grated lime rind together in a bowl, stirring well to blend thoroughly and evenly. Season to taste with salt and pepper.

3 Carefully spoon the crumb mixture over the fish pieces, pressing lightly with your hand to hold it in place.

4 Bake the dish, uncovered, in the preheated oven for 35–40 minutes, or until the fish is cooked through and the crumb topping is golden brown.

5 Serve the dish hot, garnished with lime slices and rind and accompanied by boiled new potatoes and mixed salad leaves.

COOK'S TIP

To test whether the fish is cooked through, use a fork to pierce it in the thickest part – if the flesh is white all the way through and flakes apart easily, it is cooked sufficiently.

74

spicy thai seafood stew

serves four

200 g/7 oz squid, cleaned and
tentacles discarded

500 g/1 lb 2 oz firm white fish fillet,
preferably monkfish or halibut

1 tbsp sunflower oil

4 shallots, finely chopped

2 garlic cloves, finely chopped

2 tbsp Thai green curry paste

2 small lemon grass stalks,
finely chopped

1 tsp shrimp paste

500 ml/18 fl oz coconut milk

200 g/7 oz raw tiger prawns,
peeled and deveined

12 live clams in shells, cleaned

8 fresh basil leaves, finely shredded

fresh basil leaves, to garnish

freshly cooked rice, to serve

1 Using a sharp knife, cut the squid body cavities into thick rings and the white fish into bite-sized chunks.

2 Heat the oil in a large frying pan or preheated wok. Add the shallots, garlic and curry paste and stir-fry for 1–2 minutes. Add the lemon grass and shrimp paste, stir in the coconut milk and bring to the boil.

3 Reduce the heat until the liquid is simmering gently, then add the white fish, squid and prawns to the frying pan and simmer for 2 minutes.

4 Add the clams and simmer for a further 1 minute, until the clams have opened. Discard any clams that remain closed.

5 Sprinkle the shredded basil leaves over the stew. Transfer to serving plates, garnish with whole basil leaves and serve immediately with rice.

VARIATION

If you prefer, live mussels in shells can be used instead of clams – add them after the prawns and continue as in the recipe.

spiced steamed fish

serves four–six

2.5-cm/1-inch piece fresh root
    ginger, finely grated

1 lemon grass stalk (base only),
    thinly sliced

6 fresh red chillies, deseeded and
    roughly chopped

1 small red onion, finely chopped

1 tbsp Thai fish sauce

900 g/2 lb whole fish, cleaned

2 fresh kaffir lime leaves,
    thinly sliced

2 fresh basil sprigs

TO SERVE

freshly cooked rice

cucumber, cut into matchsticks

1 Place the ginger, lemon grass, chillies, onion and fish sauce in a blender or food processor. Process to a coarse paste, adding a little water, if needed.

2 Cut 3–4 deep slits crossways on each side of the fish. Spread over the spice paste, rubbing it well into the slits. Place the fish in a dish deep enough to hold the liquid that collects during steaming. Sprinkle over the lime leaves and basil.

3 Set up a steamer or place a rack into a wok or deep pan. Bring about 5 cm/2 inches of water to the boil in the steamer or wok.

4 Place the dish of fish into the steamer or on to the rack. Reduce the heat to a simmer, cover tightly and steam the fish for 15–20 minutes, or until the fish is cooked through. Serve with freshly cooked rice and cucumber matchsticks.

COOK'S TIP

You can use any whole fish in this recipe, such as sea bass, red snapper, trout or tilapia.

pan-fried spiced salmon

serves four

2.5-cm/1-inch piece fresh root
   ginger, grated
1 tsp coriander seeds, crushed
¼ tsp chilli powder
1 tbsp lime juice
1 tsp sesame oil
4 salmon fillet pieces with skin,
   about 150 g/5½ oz each
2 tbsp vegetable oil
fresh coriander leaves, to garnish
TO SERVE
freshly cooked rice
stir-fried vegetables

1 Mix the ginger, crushed coriander, chilli powder, lime juice and sesame oil together in a bowl.

2 Place the salmon on a wide, non-metallic plate or dish and spoon the mixture over the flesh side of the fillets, spreading it to coat each piece of salmon evenly.

3 Cover the dish with clingfilm and leave to chill in the refrigerator for 30 minutes.

4 Heat a wide, heavy-based frying pan or ridged grill pan with the vegetable oil over a high heat. Place the salmon in the hot frying pan, skin-side down, and cook for 4–5 minutes, without turning, until the salmon is crusty underneath and the flesh flakes easily.

5 Serve the salmon immediately with freshly cooked rice, garnished with coriander leaves, and stir-fried vegetables.

COOK'S TIP

Use a heavy-based frying pan or solid grill pan to ensure that the fish cooks evenly throughout without sticking. If the fish is very thick, you may prefer to turn it over to cook on the other side for 2–3 minutes.

78

spiced tuna in sweet & sour sauce

serves four

4 fresh tuna steaks, about 500 g/
    1 lb 2 oz in total

$\frac{1}{4}$ tsp pepper

2 tbsp groundnut oil

1 onion, diced

1 small red pepper, deseeded and
    cut into matchsticks

1 garlic clove, crushed

$\frac{1}{2}$ cucumber, deseeded and cut
    into matchsticks

2 pineapple slices, diced

1 tsp finely chopped fresh
    root ginger

1 tbsp soft light brown sugar

1 tbsp cornflour

1$\frac{1}{2}$ tbsp lime juice

1 tbsp Thai fish sauce

250 ml/9 fl oz fish stock

TO GARNISH

lime slices

cucumber slices

COOK'S TIP

Tuna can be served quite
lightly cooked. It can be dry
if overcooked.

1 Sprinkle the tuna steaks with
pepper on both sides. Heat a
heavy-based frying pan or ridged grill
pan and brush with a little of the oil.
Arrange the tuna steaks in the frying
pan and cook for 8 minutes, turning
them over once.

2 Meanwhile, heat the remaining
oil in a separate frying pan. Add
the onion, pepper and garlic and fry
gently for 3–4 minutes to soften.

3 Remove the frying pan from the
heat and stir in the cucumber,
pineapple, ginger and sugar.

4 Blend the cornflour with the
lime juice and fish sauce, then
stir into the stock and add to the frying
pan. Stir over a medium heat until
boiling, then cook for 1–2 minutes,
until thickened and clear.

5 Spoon the sauce over the tuna
and serve immediately, garnished
with slices of lime and cucumber.

salmon with red curry in banana leaves

serves four

4 salmon steaks, about
    175 g/6 oz each
2 banana leaves, halved
1 garlic clove, crushed
1 tsp grated fresh root ginger
1 tbsp Thai red curry paste
1 tsp soft light brown sugar
1 tbsp Thai fish sauce
2 tbsp lime juice
TO GARNISH
lime wedges
whole fresh red chillies
finely chopped fresh red chilli

1 Preheat the oven to 220°C/ 425°F/Gas Mark 7. Place a salmon steak on the centre of each half banana leaf.

2 Mix the garlic, ginger, curry paste, sugar and fish sauce together, then spread over the surface of the fish. Sprinkle with lime juice.

3 Carefully wrap the banana leaves around the fish, tucking in the sides as you go to make neat, compact parcels.

4 Place the parcels seam-side down on a baking sheet and bake in the preheated oven for 15–20 minutes, or until the fish is cooked and the banana leaves are beginning to brown. Serve garnished with lime wedges, whole chillies and finely chopped chilli.

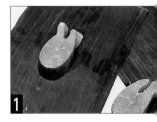

COOK'S TIP
Fresh banana leaves are often sold in packets containing several leaves, but if you buy more than you need, they will store in the refrigerator for about a week.

coconut prawns

serves four

50 g/1¾ oz desiccated coconut

25 g/1 oz fresh white breadcrumbs

1 tsp Chinese five-spice powder

½ tsp salt

finely grated rind of 1 lime

1 egg white

450 g/1 lb raw fantail prawns

sunflower or corn oil, for frying

lemon wedges, to garnish

1 Mix the desiccated coconut, breadcrumbs, Chinese five-spice powder, salt and finely grated lime rind together in a bowl.

2 Lightly whisk the egg white in a separate bowl.

3 Rinse the prawns under cold running water and pat dry with kitchen paper.

4 Dip the prawns into the egg white, then into the coconut crumb mixture, so that they are evenly coated.

5 Heat about 5 cm/2 inches of oil in a large preheated wok.

6 Add the prawns to the wok and stir-fry for 5 minutes, or until golden and crispy.

7 Remove the prawns with a slotted spoon, transfer to kitchen paper and leave to drain thoroughly.

8 Transfer the coconut prawns to warmed serving dishes and garnish with lemon wedges. Serve immediately.

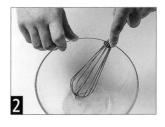

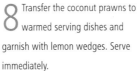

prawn skewers with tamarind glaze

serves four

1 garlic clove, chopped

1 fresh red bird's eye chilli,
    deseeded and chopped

1 tbsp tamarind paste

1 tbsp sesame oil

1 tbsp dark soy sauce

2 tbsp lime juice

1 tbsp soft light brown sugar

16 large raw tiger prawns, in shells

lime wedges, to garnish

TO SERVE

crusty bread

salad leaves

COOK'S TIP

Before using wooden or bamboo
skewers, soak them in water for
at least 30 minutes to prevent
them burning under the grill.

1 Place the garlic, chilli, tamarind
paste, sesame oil, soy sauce,
lime juice and sugar in a small
saucepan. Stir constantly over a low
heat until the sugar is dissolved, then
remove the saucepan from the heat
and leave to cool completely.

2 Rinse the prawns under cold
running water and pat dry with
kitchen paper. Arrange in a single layer
in a wide, non-metallic dish. Spoon the
marinade over the prawns and turn to
coat evenly. Cover and leave to
marinate in the refrigerator for at least
2 hours or preferably overnight.

3 Preheat the grill to medium.
Thread 4 prawns on to each
presoaked skewer and cook under the
preheated hot grill for 5–6 minutes,
turning them over once, until they turn
pink and begin to brown. Alternatively
barbecue over hot coals.

4 Thread a wedge of lime on to the
end of each skewer and serve
with crusty bread and salad leaves.

82

stir-fried squid with hot black bean sauce

serves four

750 g/1 lb 10 oz squid, cleaned and
tentacles discarded

1 large red pepper, deseeded

85 g/3 oz mangetout

1 head pak choi

3 tbsp black bean sauce

1 tbsp Thai fish sauce

1 tbsp rice wine or dry sherry

1 tbsp dark soy sauce

1 tsp soft light brown sugar

1 tsp cornflour

1 tbsp water

1 tbsp sunflower oil

1 tsp sesame oil

1 small fresh red bird's eye
chilli, chopped

1 garlic clove, finely chopped

1 tsp grated fresh root ginger

2 spring onions, chopped

COOK'S TIP

Quick stir-frying is an ideal
cooking method for squid,
because if overcooked it can
be tough. It also seals in the
colours, flavours and nutritional
value of fresh vegetables.

1 Cut the squid body cavities into quarters lengthways. Use the tip of a small, sharp knife to score a diamond pattern into the flesh, without cutting all the way through. Pat dry with kitchen paper.

2 Cut the pepper into long, thin slices. Cut the mangetout in half diagonally. Roughly shred the pak choi.

3 Mix the black bean sauce, fish sauce, rice wine, soy sauce and sugar together in a bowl. Blend the cornflour with the water and stir into the other sauce ingredients. Reserve until required.

4 Heat the oils in a preheated wok. Add the chilli, garlic, ginger and spring onions and stir-fry for 1 minute. Add the pepper slices and stir-fry for 2 minutes.

5 Add the squid and stir-fry over a high heat for a further 1 minute. Stir in the mangetout and pak choi and stir for a further 1 minute, until wilted.

6 Stir in the sauce ingredients and cook, stirring constantly, for 2 minutes, or until the sauce thickens and clears. Serve immediately.

spicy scallops with lime & chilli

serves four

16 large scallops, shelled

15 g/½ oz butter

1 tbsp vegetable oil

1 tsp crushed garlic

1 tsp grated fresh root ginger

1 bunch of spring onions,
   finely sliced

finely grated rind of 1 lime

1 small fresh red chilli, deseeded
   and very finely chopped

3 tbsp lime juice

lime wedges, to garnish

freshly cooked rice, to serve

1 Using a sharp knife, trim the scallops to remove any black intestine, then wash and pat dry with kitchen paper. Separate the corals from the white parts, then slice each white part in half horizontally, making 2 rounds.

2 Heat the butter and oil in a frying pan or preheated wok. Add the garlic and ginger and stir-fry for 1 minute without browning. Add the spring onions and stir-fry for a further 1 minute.

3 Add the scallops and continue stir-frying over a high heat for 4–5 minutes. Stir in the lime rind, chilli and lime juice and cook for a further 1 minute.

4 Transfer the scallops to serving plates, spoon over the pan juices and garnish with lime wedges. Serve hot with freshly cooked rice.

prawn & pineapple curry

serves four

½ fresh pineapple

450 ml/16 fl oz coconut cream

2 tbsp Thai red curry paste

2 tbsp Thai fish sauce

2 tsp sugar

350 g/12 oz raw tiger prawns

2 tbsp chopped fresh coriander

steamed jasmine rice, to serve

VARIATION

For an extra touch, shred
4 spring onions and sprinkle over
just before serving.

1 Peel the pineapple and chop the flesh. Heat the coconut cream, pineapple, curry paste, fish sauce and sugar until almost boiling.

2 Peel and devein the prawns. Add the prawns and coriander to the saucepan and simmer for 3 minutes, or until the prawns are cooked.

3 Serve the prawns with steamed jasmine rice.

Meat & Poultry

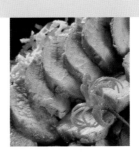

Because of the Thai Buddhist religion, which forbids the killing of animals, most butchers in Thailand are immigrant workers. Religion does not forbid eating meat, though it is often regarded as a special treat. Chicken is much more common than beef, and it's not unusual to see chicken, or sometimes pork, combined with seafood such as prawns or crabmeat – a combination which works surprisingly well. Duck, another Thai favourite, is frequently barbecue-roasted with warm spices and soy or sweet glazes, much as in the customary Chinese style.

beef & peppers with lemon grass

serves four

500 g/1 lb 2 oz lean beef fillet

2 tbsp vegetable oil

1 garlic clove, finely chopped

1 lemon grass stalk, finely shredded

2.5-cm/1-inch piece fresh root
    ginger, finely chopped

1 red pepper, deseeded and
    thickly sliced

1 green pepper, deseeded and
    thickly sliced

1 onion, thickly sliced

2 tbsp lime juice

salt and pepper

freshly cooked noodles or rice,
    to serve

1 Cut the beef into long, thin strips,
cutting across the grain.

2 Heat the oil in a large frying pan
or preheated wok over a high
heat. Add the garlic and stir-fry for
1 minute.

3 Add the beef and stir-fry for a
further 2–3 minutes, or until
lightly coloured. Stir in the lemon grass
and ginger and remove the frying pan
from the heat.

4 Remove the beef from the frying
pan and reserve. Next add the
peppers and onion to the frying
pan and stir-fry over a high heat for
2–3 minutes, or until the onions
are just turning golden brown and
slightly softened.

5 Return the beef to the frying pan,
stir in the lime juice and season to
taste with salt and pepper. Serve with
freshly cooked noodles or rice.

beef & coconut curry

serves four

800 g/1 lb 12 oz braising steak

3 tbsp vegetable oil

2 onions, thinly sliced

2 tbsp Thai red curry paste

1 tbsp tamarind paste or lime juice

2 tbsp Thai fish sauce

850 ml/1½ pints coconut milk

2 tsp sugar

6 cardamom pods, crushed

1 small pineapple, peeled
  and chopped

TO SERVE

freshly cooked rice

prawn crackers

4 Simmer gently, uncovered, for 1–1½ hours, or until the beef is tender. Stir from time to time, and if it is becoming dry, cover with a lid.

3 Stir in the tamarind paste, fish sauce, coconut milk and sugar. Bring to the boil, then reduce the heat and return the beef and onions to the casserole with the cardamom.

5 Add the pineapple and cook for a further 5 minutes. The curry should be quite dry, but add a little water if necessary.

6 Serve immediately with rice and prawn crackers.

1 Cut the beef into cubes. Heat the oil in a flameproof casserole. Brown the beef in batches and reserve.

2 Add the onions to the oil and cook for 5 minutes, then reserve with the beef. Add the curry paste and cook gently for 1 minute, stirring constantly.

stir-fried beef with beansprouts

serves four

1 bunch of spring onions

2 tbsp sunflower oil

1 garlic clove, crushed

1 tsp finely chopped fresh
  root ginger

500 g/1 lb 2 oz tender beef fillet,
  cut into thin strips

1 large red pepper, deseeded
  and sliced

1 small fresh red chilli, deseeded
  and chopped

350 g/12 oz fresh beansprouts

1 small lemon grass stalk,
  finely chopped

25 g/1 oz smooth peanut butter

4 tbsp coconut milk

1 tbsp rice vinegar or white
  wine vinegar

1 tbsp soy sauce

1 tsp soft light brown sugar

250 g/9 oz medium egg noodles

salt and pepper

1 Thinly slice the spring onions, reserving some slices to use as a garnish.

2 Heat the oil in a frying pan or preheated wok over a high heat. Add the spring onions, garlic and ginger and stir-fry for 2–3 minutes to soften. Add the beef and continue stir-frying for 4–5 minutes, until evenly browned.

COOK'S TIP

When preparing lemon grass, take care to remove the outer layers, which can be tough and fibrous. Use only the tender part at the centre, which has the finest flavour.

3 Add the pepper and stir-fry for a further 3–4 minutes. Add the chilli and beansprouts and stir-fry for 2 minutes. Mix the lemon grass, peanut butter, coconut milk, rice vinegar, soy sauce and sugar together in a bowl, then stir into the frying pan.

4 Meanwhile, cook the egg noodles in boiling salted water for 4 minutes, or according to the packet instructions. Drain and stir into the frying pan, tossing to mix evenly.

5 Season to taste with salt and pepper. Sprinkle with the reserved spring onions and serve hot.

red-hot beef with cashew nuts

serves four

500 g/1 lb 2 oz lean boneless
   beef sirloin

1 tsp vegetable oil

MARINADE

1 tbsp sesame seeds

1 garlic clove, chopped

1 tbsp finely chopped fresh
   root ginger

1 fresh red bird's eye chilli, chopped

2 tbsp dark soy sauce

1 tsp Thai red curry paste

TO FINISH

1 tsp sesame oil

4 tbsp unsalted cashew nuts

1 spring onion, thickly
   sliced diagonally

cucumber slices, to garnish

1 Using a sharp knife, cut the beef into 1-cm/½-inch wide strips. Place them in a large, non-metallic bowl.

2 To make the marinade, toast the sesame seeds in a heavy-based frying pan over a medium heat for 2–3 minutes, until golden brown, shaking the frying pan occasionally.

3 Place the seeds in a mortar with the garlic, ginger and chilli and, using a pestle, grind to a smooth paste. Add the soy sauce and curry paste and mix well.

4 Spoon the paste over the beef strips and toss to coat the meat evenly. Cover and leave to marinate in the refrigerator for at least 2–3 hours or overnight.

5 Heat a heavy-based frying pan or ridged grill pan until very hot and brush with vegetable oil. Place the beef strips in the frying pan and cook quickly, turning frequently, until lightly browned. Remove the frying pan from the heat and spoon the beef into a pile on a hot serving dish.

6 Heat the sesame oil in a small frying pan. Add the cashew nuts and quickly fry until golden. Add the spring onion and stir-fry for 30 seconds. Sprinkle the mixture on top of the beef strips, garnish with cucumber slices and serve immediately.

94

beef satay with peanut sauce

serves four

500 g/1 lb 2 oz lean beef fillet

2 garlic cloves, crushed

2-cm/¾-inch piece fresh root ginger, finely grated

1 tbsp soft light brown sugar

1 tbsp dark soy sauce

1 tbsp lime juice

2 tsp sesame oil

1 tsp ground coriander

1 tsp ground turmeric

½ tsp chilli powder

PEANUT SAUCE

300 ml/10 fl oz coconut milk

8 tbsp crunchy peanut butter

½ small onion, grated

2 tsp soft light brown sugar

½ tsp chilli powder

1 tbsp dark soy sauce

TO GARNISH

chopped cucumber

red pepper pieces

1 Cut the beef into 1-cm/½-inch cubes and place in a large bowl.

2 Add the garlic, ginger, sugar, soy sauce, lime juice, sesame oil, coriander, turmeric and chilli powder. Mix well to coat the pieces of meat evenly. Cover and leave to marinate in the refrigerator for at least 2 hours or overnight.

COOK'S TIP

Make sure the grill or barbecue is very hot before you begin to cook. Soak the skewers in cold water for 20 minutes before using to reduce the risk of the skewers burning. For an elegant presentation, serve the sauce in a large lettuce leaf, garnished with snipped fresh chives.

3 Preheat the grill to high. To make the peanut sauce, place all the ingredients in a small saucepan and stir over a medium heat until boiling. Remove the saucepan from the heat and keep warm.

4 Thread the beef cubes onto presoaked bamboo skewers. Cook the skewers under the hot grill for 3–5 minutes, turning frequently, until golden. Alternatively, barbecue over hot coals. Transfer to a large serving plate, garnish with chopped cucumber and red pepper pieces and serve with the peanut sauce.

hot beef & coconut curry

serves four

400 ml/14 fl oz coconut milk

2 tbsp Thai red curry paste

2 garlic cloves, crushed

500 g/1 lb 2 oz braising steak

2 fresh kaffir lime leaves, shredded

3 tbsp lime juice

2 tbsp Thai fish sauce

1 large fresh red chilli, deseeded
   and sliced

½ tsp ground turmeric

salt and pepper

2 tbsp chopped fresh basil leaves

2 tbsp chopped fresh
   coriander leaves

shredded coconut, to garnish

freshly cooked rice, to serve

1 Place the coconut milk in a large saucepan and bring to the boil. Reduce the heat and simmer gently for 10 minutes, or until it has thickened. Stir in the curry paste and garlic and simmer for a further 5 minutes.

2 Cut the beef into 2-cm/¾-inch chunks. Add to the saucepan and bring to the boil, stirring constantly. Reduce the heat and add the lime leaves, lime juice, fish sauce, sliced chilli, turmeric and ½ teaspoon of salt.

3 Cover the saucepan and continue simmering for 20–25 minutes, or until the meat is tender, adding a little water if the sauce looks too dry.

COOK'S TIP

This recipe uses one of the larger, milder red chilli peppers – either fresno or Dutch – simply because they give more colour to the dish. If you prefer to use small bird's eye chillies, you'll need only one because they are much hotter. For an elegant presentation, garnish the rice with a few strips of fresh red chilli.

4 Stir in the basil and coriander and season to taste with salt and pepper. Sprinkle with shredded coconut and serve with freshly cooked rice.

spicy fried minced pork

serves four

2 garlic cloves

3 shallots

2.5-cm/1-inch piece fresh
   root ginger

2 tbsp sunflower oil

500 g/1 lb 2 oz lean pork mince

2 tbsp Thai fish sauce

1 tbsp dark soy sauce

1 tbsp Thai red curry paste

4 dried kaffir lime leaves, crumbled

4 plum tomatoes, chopped

3 tbsp chopped fresh coriander

salt and pepper

freshly cooked fine egg noodles,
   to serve

TO GARNISH

fresh coriander sprigs

spring onion tassels (see Cook's Tip)

1 Finely chop the garlic, shallots and ginger. Heat the oil in a large frying pan or preheated wok over a medium heat. Add the garlic, shallots and ginger and stir-fry for 2 minutes. Stir in the pork and continue stir-frying until golden brown.

2 Stir in the fish sauce, soy sauce, curry paste and lime leaves and stir-fry for a further 1–2 minutes over a high heat.

3 Add the chopped tomatoes and cook for a further 5–6 minutes, stirring occasionally. Stir in the chopped coriander and season to taste with salt and pepper.

4 Serve hot, spooned on to freshly cooked fine egg noodles, garnished with coriander sprigs and spring onion tassels.

COOK'S TIP

To make the spring onion tassels, make a few cuts lengthways down the stem of each spring onion. Place in a bowl of ice-cold water and leave until the tassels open out. Drain well before using.

roasted red pork

serves four

600 g/1 lb 5 oz pork fillets

Chinese leaves, shredded

1 fresh red chilli flower (see page 160), to garnish

MARINADE

2 garlic cloves, crushed

1 tbsp grated fresh root ginger

1 tbsp light soy sauce

1 tbsp Thai fish sauce

1 tbsp rice wine or dry sherry

1 tbsp hoisin sauce

1 tbsp sesame oil

1 tbsp palm sugar or soft brown sugar

½ tsp Chinese five-spice powder

few drops of red food colouring (optional)

1 Mix all the ingredients for the marinade together in a small bowl, then spread over the pork, turning to coat evenly. Place in a large, non-metallic dish, cover and leave to marinate in the refrigerator overnight.

2 Preheat the oven to 220°C/425°F/ Gas Mark 7. Place a rack in a roasting tin, then half fill the tin with boiling water. Lift the pork from the marinade and place on the rack. Reserve the marinade.

VARIATION

The pork may also be grilled. Cut the meat into slices or strips and coat in the marinade, then arrange on a foil-lined grill pan and grill under a high heat, turning occasionally and basting with the marinade.

3 Roast in the preheated oven for 20 minutes. Baste with the marinade, then reduce the heat to 180°C/350°F/Gas Mark 4 and continue roasting for a further 35–40 minutes, basting occasionally with the marinade, until the pork is a rich, reddish brown and thoroughly cooked.

4 Cut the pork into slices and arrange on a bed of shredded Chinese leaves. Garnish with a red chilli flower and serve.

pork steaks with lemon grass

serves four

2 lemon grass stalks, outer
   leaves removed

2 garlic cloves, crushed

½ tsp pepper

1 tbsp sugar

2 tbsp Thai fish sauce

2 tbsp soy sauce

1 tbsp sesame oil

1 tbsp lime juice

4 spring onions, finely chopped

2 tbsp coconut milk

4 pork steaks

lime wedges, to garnish

VARIATION

The pork steaks are perfect for
cooking over medium–hot coals
on the barbecue.

---

1 Finely chop the lemon grass and
place in a bowl with the garlic,
pepper, sugar, fish sauce, soy sauce,
oil, lime juice, spring onions and
coconut milk. Mix well to combine.

2 Place the pork steaks in a large,
shallow, non-metallic dish. Pour
over the marinade and turn the steaks
until coated. Cover the dish with
clingfilm and leave to marinate in the
refrigerator for 1 hour.

3 Preheat the grill to medium.
Cook the pork steaks under the
hot grill for 5 minutes on each side,
or until cooked through. Garnish with
lime wedges and serve immediately.

stir-fried pork & sweetcorn

serves four

2 tbsp vegetable oil

500 g/1 lb 2 oz lean boneless pork,
   cut into thin strips

1 garlic clove, chopped

350 g/12 oz fresh sweetcorn kernels

200 g/7 oz French beans, cut into
   short lengths

2 spring onions, chopped

1 small fresh red chilli, chopped

1 tsp sugar

1 tbsp light soy sauce

3 tbsp chopped fresh coriander

freshly cooked egg noodles or rice,
   to serve

COOK'S TIP

In Thailand, long beans would be
used for dishes such as this, but
you can substitute French beans,
which are more easily available.
Look out for long beans in Thai
food shops – they are like long
string beans and have a similar
flavour, but their texture is crisp,
and they cook more quickly.

1 Heat the oil in a large frying pan
or preheated wok. Add the pork
and stir-fry quickly over a high heat
until lightly browned.

2 Stir in the garlic, sweetcorn,
beans, spring onions and chilli
and continue stir-frying over a high
heat for 2–3 minutes, until the
vegetables are heated through and
almost tender.

3 Stir in the sugar and soy sauce
and stir-fry for a further
30 seconds over a high heat.

4 Sprinkle with the coriander and
serve immediately with freshly
cooked egg noodles or rice.

104

pork with soy & sesame glaze

serves four

2 pork fillets, about
275 g/9½ oz each

2 tbsp dark soy sauce

2 tbsp clear honey

2 garlic cloves, crushed

1 tbsp sesame seeds

1 onion, thinly sliced into rings

1 tbsp plain flour, seasoned

sunflower oil, for frying

crisp salad leaves, to serve

1 Preheat the oven to
200°C/400°F/Gas Mark 6. Trim
the pork fillets and place in a wide,
non-metallic dish.

2 Mix the soy sauce, honey and
garlic together in a small bowl,
then spread over the pork, turning to
coat evenly.

3 Lift the pork fillets into a roasting
tin or shallow ovenproof dish and
sprinkle evenly with sesame seeds.

4 Roast the pork in the preheated
oven for 20 minutes, spooning
over any juices. Cover loosely with foil
to prevent overbrowning and roast for
a further 10–15 minutes, or until the
meat is thoroughly cooked.

5 Meanwhile, dip the onion slices
in the seasoned flour and shake
off the excess. Heat the oil in a small
frying pan. Add the onion rings and fry
until golden and crisp, turning
occasionally. Serve the pork in slices
with the fried onions on a bed of crisp
salad leaves.

tamarind pork

serves four

2 tbsp vegetable oil

600 g/1 lb 5 oz lean boneless pork,
    cut into thin strips

225 g/8 oz canned bamboo
    shoots, drained

freshly cooked noodles, to serve

SPICE PASTE

2.5-cm/1-inch piece fresh
    root ginger

4 shallots, finely chopped

2 garlic cloves, finely chopped

1 tsp ground coriander

2 fresh red chillies, deseeded and
    finely chopped

½ tsp ground turmeric

6 blanched almonds, finely chopped

2 tbsp tamarind paste

2 tbsp hot water

1 To make the spice paste, peel the ginger and finely chop. Place the shallots, garlic, ginger, coriander, chillies, turmeric, almonds, tamarind paste and water in a food processor and process until smooth.

2 Heat the oil in a preheated wok or frying pan over a high heat. Add the pork and cook for 3 minutes, or until the meat is coloured. Add the spice paste and continue to cook for a further 2–3 minutes.

3 Add the bamboo shoots and cook for a further 2 minutes, or until the pork is cooked through. Serve with freshly cooked noodles.

VARIATION
If you cannot find shallots,
replace them with
ordinary small onions.

106

spiced pork sausages

serves four

400 g/14 oz lean pork mince

50 g/1¾ oz cooked rice

1 garlic clove, crushed

1 tsp Thai red curry paste

1 tsp pepper

1 tsp ground coriander

½ tsp salt

3 tbsp lime juice

2 tbsp chopped fresh coriander

3 tbsp groundnut oil

Chilli & Coconut Sambal (see page 176) or soy sauce, to serve

TO GARNISH

cucumber slices

fresh red chilli strips

3 Heat the oil in a large frying pan over a medium heat. Add the sausages, in batches if necessary, and fry for 8–10 minutes, turning them over occasionally, until they are evenly golden brown and cooked through. Transfer to a serving plate, garnish with cucumber slices and a few strips of red chilli and serve hot with Chilli & Coconut Sambal or soy sauce.

COOK'S TIP

These sausages can also be served as a starter – shape the mixture slightly smaller to make 16 bite-sized sausages. Serve with a soy dipping sauce.

1 Place the pork, rice, garlic, curry paste, pepper, ground coriander, salt, lime juice and chopped coriander in a bowl and knead together with your hands to mix evenly.

2 Use your hands to form the mixture into 12 small sausage shapes. Using sausage casings, if available, will help to keep the sausages together when cooked.

108

thai-style burgers

serves four

1 small lemon grass stalk

1 small fresh red chilli, deseeded

2 garlic cloves

2 spring onions

200 g/7 oz closed-cup mushrooms

400 g/14 oz lean pork mince

1 tbsp Thai fish sauce

3 tbsp chopped fresh coriander

salt and pepper

plain flour, for dusting

sunflower oil, for shallow-frying

2 tbsp mayonnaise

1 tbsp lime juice

TO SERVE

4 sesame hamburger buns

shredded Chinese leaves

COOK'S TIP

You can add a spoonful of your favourite relish to each burger, or add a few Crisp Pickled Vegetables (see page 166) for a change of texture.

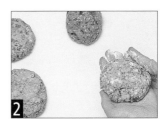

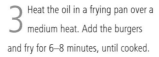

1 Place the lemon grass, chilli, garlic and spring onions in a food processor and process to a smooth paste. Add the mushrooms and process until very finely chopped.

2 Add the pork, fish sauce and coriander. Season well with salt and pepper, then divide the mixture into 4 equal portions and form into flat burger shapes with lightly floured hands.

3 Heat the oil in a frying pan over a medium heat. Add the burgers and fry for 6–8 minutes, until cooked.

4 Meanwhile, mix the mayonnaise with the lime juice in a small bowl. Split the hamburger buns and spread the lime-flavoured mayonnaise on the cut surfaces. Add a few shredded Chinese leaves, top with a burger, sandwich together and serve.

lamb with lime leaves

2 fresh red bird's eye chillies

2 tbsp groundnut oil

2 garlic cloves, crushed

4 shallots, chopped

2 stalks lemon grass, sliced

6 fresh kaffir lime leaves

1 tbsp tamarind paste

25 g/1 oz palm sugar

450 g/1 lb lean lamb (leg or
loin fillet)

600 ml/1 pint coconut milk

175 g/6 oz cherry tomatoes, halved

1 tbsp chopped fresh coriander

freshly cooked Thai fragrant rice,
to serve

1 Using a sharp knife, deseed and very finely chop the chillies. Reserve until required.

2 Heat the oil in a large preheated wok. Add the garlic, shallots, lemon grass, lime leaves, tamarind paste, sugar and chillies to the wok and stir-fry for 2 minutes.

3 Using a sharp knife, cut the lamb into thin strips or cubes.

4 Add the lamb to the wok and stir-fry for 5 minutes, tossing well so that the lamb is evenly coated in the spice mixture.

5 Pour the coconut milk into the wok and bring to the boil. Reduce the heat and leave to simmer for 20 minutes.

6 Add the cherry tomatoes and chopped coriander to the wok and simmer for 5 minutes. Transfer to serving plates and serve hot with fragrant rice.

COOK'S TIP

Groundnut oil is used here
for flavour – it is an oil
commonly used for stir-frying.

red lamb curry

serves four

500 g/1 lb 2 oz lean, boneless
  leg of lamb
2 tbsp vegetable oil
1 large onion, sliced
2 garlic cloves, crushed
2 tbsp Thai red curry paste
150 ml/5 fl oz coconut milk
1 tbsp soft light brown sugar
1 large red pepper, deseeded and
  thickly sliced
125 ml/4 fl oz lamb or beef stock
1 tbsp Thai fish sauce
2 tbsp lime juice
225 g/8 oz canned
  water chestnuts, drained
2 tbsp chopped fresh coriander
2 tbsp chopped fresh basil
salt and pepper
fresh basil leaves, to garnish
freshly cooked jasmine rice, to serve

VARIATION

This curry can also be made with other lean red meats. Try replacing the lamb with trimmed duck breasts or pieces of lean braising beef. This richly spiced curry uses the typically red-hot chilli flavour of Thai red curry paste, made with dried red chillies, to give it a warm, russet-red colour.

1 Trim the meat and cut it into 3-cm/1¼-inch cubes. Heat the oil in a large frying pan or preheated wok over a high heat. Add the onion and garlic and stir-fry for 2–3 minutes to soften. Add the meat and stir-fry the mixture quickly until lightly browned.

2 Stir in the curry paste and cook for a few seconds, then add the coconut milk and sugar and bring to the boil. Reduce the heat and simmer for 15 minutes, stirring occasionally.

3 Stir in the red pepper, stock, fish sauce and lime juice, cover and simmer for a further 15 minutes, or until the meat is tender.

4 Add the water chestnuts, coriander and basil and season to taste with salt and pepper. Transfer to serving plates, garnish with basil leaves and serve with jasmine rice.

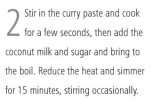

112

stir-fried lamb with mint

serves four

25 g/1 oz fresh mint leaves

2 tbsp vegetable oil

2 garlic cloves, finely sliced

2 fresh red chillies, deseeded and
cut into thin strips

1 onion, thinly sliced

1½ tbsp Madras curry paste

500 g/1 lb 2 oz lamb fillet, cut
into thin strips

225 g/8 oz canned baby
corn cobs, drained

4 spring onions, finely chopped

1 tbsp Thai fish sauce

freshly cooked rice, to serve

VARIATION

You can use fresh baby corn
cobs, halved, instead of
canned ones, if you prefer.

---

1 Roughly shred the mint leaves
and reserve until required. Heat
half the oil in a preheated wok or large
frying pan. Add the garlic and chillies
and cook until soft. Remove and
reserve. Add the onion and cook
for 5 minutes, or until soft. Remove
and reserve.

2 Heat the remaining oil in the wok.
Add the curry paste and cook for
1 minute. Add the lamb, in batches if
necessary, and cook for 5–8 minutes,
or until cooked through and tender.

3 Return the onion to the wok with
the baby corn cobs, spring
onions, mint and fish sauce. Cook until
heated through. Sprinkle the garlic and
chillies over and serve with rice.

roast chicken with ginger & lime

serves four

3-cm/1¼-inch piece fresh root
  ginger, finely chopped

2 garlic cloves, finely chopped

1 small onion, finely chopped

1 lemon grass stalk, finely chopped

½ tsp salt

1 tsp black peppercorns

1.5 kg/3 lb 5 oz roasting chicken

1 tbsp coconut cream

2 tbsp lime juice

2 tbsp clear honey

1 tsp cornflour

2 tsp water

stir-fried vegetables, to serve

1 Place the ginger, garlic, onion, lemon grass, salt and peppercorns in a mortar and, using a pestle, crush to a smooth paste.

2 Using poultry shears or strong kitchen scissors, cut the chicken in half lengthways. Spread the paste all over the chicken, both inside and out, and spread it on to the flesh under the breast skin. Cover and leave to chill in the refrigerator for at least several hours or overnight.

3 Preheat the oven to 180°C/350°F/Gas Mark 4. Heat the coconut cream, lime juice and honey together in a small saucepan, stirring until smooth. Brush a little of the mixture evenly over the chicken.

4 Place the chicken halves on a tray over a roasting tin half-filled with boiling water. Roast in the preheated oven for 1 hour, or until the chicken is a rich golden brown colour, basting occasionally with the lime and honey mixture.

5 When the chicken is cooked, boil the water from the roasting tin to reduce it to 100 ml/3½ fl oz. Blend the cornflour and water together and stir into the reduced liquid. Bring gently to the boil, then stir until slightly thickened and clear. Serve the chicken with the sauce and freshly cooked stir-fried vegetables.

red chicken with cherry tomatoes

serves four

1 tbsp sunflower oil

450 g/1 lb skinless, boneless
   chicken breasts

2 garlic cloves, crushed

2 tbsp Thai red curry paste

2 tbsp grated fresh galangal or
   root ginger

1 tbsp tamarind paste

4 fresh kaffir lime leaves

225 g/8 oz sweet potato

600 ml/1 pint coconut milk

225 g/8 oz cherry tomatoes, halved

3 tbsp chopped fresh coriander

freshly cooked jasmine or Thai
   fragrant rice, to serve

1 Heat the oil in a large
preheated wok.

2 Using a sharp knife, thinly slice
the chicken. Add the chicken to
the wok and stir-fry for 5 minutes.

3 Add the garlic, curry paste,
galangal, tamarind paste and
lime leaves to the wok and stir-fry
for 1 minute.

4 Using a sharp knife, peel and dice
the sweet potato.

5 Add the coconut milk and sweet
potato to the mixture in the wok
and bring to the boil. Leave to bubble
over a medium heat for 20 minutes,
or until the juices begin to thicken
and reduce.

6 Add the cherry tomatoes and
coriander to the curry and cook
for a further 5 minutes, stirring
occasionally. Transfer to serving plates
and serve hot with jasmine or Thai
fragrant rice.

green chicken curry

serves four

6 skinless, boneless chicken thighs

400 ml/14 fl oz coconut milk

2 garlic cloves, crushed

2 tbsp Thai fish sauce

2 tbsp Thai green curry paste

12 baby aubergines

3 fresh green chillies, finely chopped

3 fresh kaffir lime leaves, shredded,
    plus extra to garnish (optional)

salt and pepper

4 tbsp chopped fresh coriander

freshly cooked rice, to serve

1 Cut the chicken into bite-sized pieces. Pour the coconut milk into a preheated wok or large frying pan over a high heat and bring to the boil.

2 Add the chicken, garlic and fish sauce to the wok and return to the boil. Reduce the heat and simmer gently for 30 minutes, or until the chicken is just tender.

3 Remove the chicken from the wok with a slotted spoon. Keep warm.

4 Stir the curry paste into the wok, add the aubergines, chillies and lime leaves and simmer for 5 minutes.

5 Return the chicken to the wok and bring to the boil. Season to taste with salt and pepper, then stir in the coriander. Transfer to serving plates, garnish with lime leaves, if using, and serve immediately with freshly cooked rice.

COOK'S TIP

Baby aubergines, or 'pea aubergines' as they are called in Thailand, are traditionally used in this curry, but they are not always available. If you can't find them in a Thai food shop, use chopped ordinary aubergine, or substitute a few green peas.

118

chicken & mango stir-fry

serves four

6 skinless, boneless chicken thighs

2.5-cm/1-inch piece fresh root
　ginger, grated

1 garlic clove, crushed

1 small fresh red chilli, deseeded
　and chopped

1 large red pepper, deseeded

4 spring onions

200 g/7 oz mangetout

100 g/3½ oz baby corn cobs

1 large firm, ripe mango

2 tbsp sunflower oil

1 tbsp light soy sauce

3 tbsp rice wine or dry sherry

1 tsp sesame oil

salt and pepper

snipped fresh chives, to garnish

1 Cut the chicken into long, thin strips and place in a bowl. Mix the ginger, garlic and chilli together in a separate bowl, then stir into the chicken strips to coat them evenly.

2 Slice the pepper thinly, cutting diagonally. Diagonally slice the spring onions. Cut the mangetout and baby corn cobs in half diagonally. Peel the mango, remove the stone and slice the flesh thinly.

3 Heat the sunflower oil in a large frying pan or preheated wok over a high heat.

4 Add the chicken and stir-fry for 4–5 minutes, until just turning golden brown. Add the pepper and stir-fry over a medium heat for 4–5 minutes, until soft.

5 Add the spring onions, mangetout and baby corn cobs and stir-fry for a further 1 minute.

6 Mix the soy sauce, rice wine and sesame oil together in a small bowl and stir it into the frying pan. Add the mango and stir gently for 1 minute to heat thoroughly. Season to taste with salt and pepper and serve immediately, garnished with snipped chives.

stir-fried chicken with thai basil

serves four

600 g/1 lb 5 oz skinless, boneless
   chicken breasts

2 tbsp vegetable oil

4 garlic cloves, crushed

4 spring onions, finely chopped

4 fresh green chillies, deseeded and
   finely chopped

1 green pepper, deseeded and
   thinly sliced

25 g/1 oz fresh Thai basil leaves,
   roughly chopped

2 tbsp Thai fish sauce

fresh basil leaves, to garnish

freshly cooked rice, to serve

1 Using a sharp knife, cut the chicken into thin strips.

2 Heat the oil in a preheated wok. Add the garlic and spring onions and cook for 2 minutes. Add the chillies and pepper and cook for a further 2 minutes.

3 Add the chicken and cook until browned. Stir in the basil and fish sauce, and stir-fry until the chicken is cooked through. Garnish with basil leaves and serve with rice.

COOK'S TIP
Thai basil is available in Thai food shops. If you cannot find it, omit it from the recipe.

chicken with lemon grass & chilli

serves four

2 fresh red chillies

2 tbsp vegetable oil

4 garlic cloves, thinly sliced

1 onion, thinly sliced

2 lemon grass stalks, outer part
   removed, very finely chopped

8 chicken thighs with bones
   and skin

3 tbsp Thai fish sauce

1 tbsp light brown sugar

225 ml/8 fl oz chicken stock

COOK'S TIP

If the chicken mixture becomes
too dry during cooking, add a
little water.

1 Using a small knife, deseed and finely chop the chillies. Heat the oil in a large frying pan. Add the garlic and onion and cook gently for 5–10 minutes, or until soft.

2 Add the lemon grass and chillies and cook for 2 minutes. Add the chicken and cook for 5 minutes, or until browned all over.

3 Add the fish sauce, sugar and stock. Bring to the boil, reduce the heat and simmer, covered, for 30 minutes, or until the chicken is cooked through. Serve immediately.

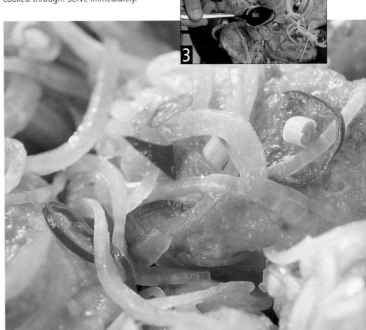

spiced coriander chicken

serves four

4 skinless, boneless chicken breasts

2 garlic cloves

1 fresh green chilli, deseeded

2-cm/$\frac{3}{4}$-inch piece fresh root ginger

4 tbsp chopped fresh coriander

finely grated rind of 1 lime

3 tbsp lime juice

2 tbsp light soy sauce

1 tbsp caster sugar

175 ml/6 fl oz coconut milk

freshly cooked rice, to serve

TO GARNISH

finely chopped fresh coriander

cucumber slices

radish slices

$\frac{1}{2}$ fresh red chilli, deseeded and
  sliced into rings

1 Using a sharp knife, cut 3 deep slashes into the skinned side of each chicken breast. Place the breasts in a single layer in a non-metallic dish.

2 Place the garlic, chilli, ginger, coriander, lime rind and juice, soy sauce, sugar and coconut milk in a food processor and process to a smooth purée.

3 Spread the purée over both sides of the chicken breasts, coating them evenly. Cover with clingfilm and leave to marinate in the refrigerator for 1 hour.

4 Preheat the grill to medium. Lift the chicken from the marinade, drain off the excess and place on a grill pan. Cook under the hot grill for 12–15 minutes, until thoroughly and evenly cooked.

5 Meanwhile, place the remaining marinade in a saucepan and bring to the boil. Reduce the heat and simmer for several minutes. Transfer the chicken breasts to serving plates, garnish with chopped coriander, cucumber slices, radish slices and chilli rings and serve with rice.

quick green chicken curry

serves four

6 spring onions

1 tbsp vegetable oil

600 g/1 lb 5oz skinless, boneless
    chicken breasts, cut into cubes

200 ml/7 fl oz coconut cream

3 tbsp Thai green curry paste

3 tbsp chopped fresh coriander

freshly cooked noodles, to serve

COOK'S TIP

Store spring onions in the salad
compartment of the refrigerator.
They will keep for up to 3 days.

1 Using a small knife, slice the
spring onions. Heat the oil in a
large frying pan. Add the spring onions
and the chicken and cook, stirring
constantly, for 3–4 minutes, or until the
chicken is browned.

2 Stir in the coconut cream and
curry paste and cook for a further
5 minutes, or until the chicken is
cooked through. Add a little water or
stock if the sauce becomes too thick.

3 Stir in the chopped coriander
and serve immediately with
freshly cooked noodles.

126

braised chicken with garlic & spices

serves four

4 garlic cloves, chopped

4 shallots, chopped

2 small fresh red chillies, deseeded
    and chopped

1 lemon grass stalk, finely chopped

1 tbsp chopped fresh coriander

1 tsp shrimp paste

½ tsp ground cinnamon

1 tbsp tamarind paste

2 tbsp vegetable oil

8 small chicken joints, such as
    drumsticks or thighs

300 ml/10 fl oz chicken stock

1 tbsp Thai fish sauce

1 tbsp smooth peanut butter

salt and pepper

4 tbsp toasted peanuts, chopped

TO SERVE

stir-fried vegetables

freshly cooked noodles

1 Place the garlic, shallots, chillies,
lemon grass, coriander and
shrimp paste in a mortar and, using a
pestle, grind to an almost smooth
paste. Add the cinnamon and tamarind
paste to the mixture.

2 Heat the oil in a wide frying pan
or preheated wok. Add the
chicken joints, turning frequently, until
golden brown on all sides. Remove the
chicken from the frying pan and keep
hot. Tip away any excess fat.

3 Add the spice paste to the frying
pan and stir over a medium heat
until lightly browned. Stir in the stock,
then return the chicken joints to the
frying pan.

4 Bring to the boil, then cover
tightly, reduce the heat and leave
to simmer for 25–30 minutes, stirring
occasionally, until the chicken is tender
and thoroughly cooked. Stir in the fish
sauce and peanut butter and simmer
for a further 10 minutes.

5 Season to taste with salt and
pepper and sprinkle the toasted
peanuts over the chicken. Serve hot
with stir-fried vegetables and noodles.

128

peanut-crusted chicken

serves six

2 garlic cloves, crushed

2.5-cm/1-inch piece fresh root
   ginger, finely grated

1 lemon grass stalk, outer leaves
   removed, finely chopped

2 tbsp chopped fresh
   coriander leaves

175 g/6 oz salted peanuts

115 g/4 oz plain flour

2 eggs

4 tbsp milk

12 chicken drumsticks, skin removed

DIPPING SAUCE

1 fresh red chilli, deseeded and
   finely chopped

2 garlic cloves, crushed

125 ml/4 fl oz white wine vinegar

2 tbsp dark brown sugar

1 Preheat the oven to 220°C/
425°F/Gas Mark 7. Place the
garlic, ginger, lemon grass, coriander
leaves, peanuts and 2 tablespoons
of the flour in a food processor and
process until finely ground. Transfer
to a shallow dish.

2 Beat the eggs and milk together
in a bowl. Spread the remaining
flour on a plate. Dip the drumsticks
into the flour, then into the egg mixture
and finally into the peanut mixture.
Arrange them in an oiled roasting tin.

3 Bake in the preheated oven for
15 minutes, then turn them and
cook for a further 15 minutes. Pour off
any excess oil and cook the drumsticks
for 5 minutes, or until very crisp.

4 To make the sauce, place the chilli
and garlic in a mortar and, using
a pestle, grind to a paste. Place the
vinegar and sugar in a saucepan and
heat gently until the sugar dissolves.
Bring to the boil and simmer for 2
minutes. Stir in the chilli paste. Transfer
to a bowl. Drain the drumsticks on
kitchen paper and serve with the sauce.

duck breasts with chilli & lime

serves four

4 boneless duck breasts

2 garlic cloves, crushed

4 tsp soft light brown sugar

3 tbsp lime juice

1 tbsp soy sauce

1 tsp chilli sauce

1 tsp vegetable oil

2 tbsp plum jam

125 ml/4 fl oz chicken stock

salt and pepper

TO SERVE

freshly cooked rice

crisp salad leaves

1 Using a small, sharp knife, cut deep slashes in the skin of the duck to make a diamond pattern. Place the duck breasts in a wide, non-metallic dish.

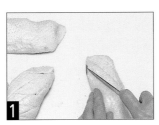

2 Mix the garlic, sugar, lime juice, and soy and chilli sauces together in a bowl, then spoon over the duck breasts, turning well to coat evenly. Cover and leave to marinate in the refrigerator for at least 3 hours or overnight.

3 Drain the duck, reserving the marinade. Heat a large, heavy-based frying pan until very hot and brush with the oil. Add the duck breasts, skin-side down, and cook for 5 minutes, or until the skin is browned and crisp. Tip away the excess fat. Turn the duck breasts over.

4 Continue cooking on the other side for 2–3 minutes to brown. Add the reserved marinade, plum jam and stock and simmer for 2 minutes. Season to taste with salt and pepper. Transfer to individual serving plates, spoon over the pan juices and serve hot with freshly cooked rice and crisp salad leaves.

131

roasted duckling with pineapple & coconut

serves four

1.6 kg/3 lb 8 oz duckling

salt and pepper

2 tbsp groundnut oil

1 small pineapple

1 large onion, chopped

1 garlic clove, finely chopped

1 tsp finely chopped fresh
   root ginger

½ tsp ground coriander

1 tbsp Thai green curry paste

1 tsp soft light brown sugar

450 ml/16 fl oz coconut milk

fresh coriander, chopped

fresh red and green chilli flowers,
   to garnish (see page 160)

freshly cooked jasmine rice, to serve

1 Preheat the grill to medium. Using a large knife or poultry shears, cut the duckling in half lengthways, cutting through the line of the breastbone. Wipe inside and out with kitchen paper. Sprinkle with salt and pepper to taste, prick the skin with a fork and brush with oil.

2 Place the duckling, cut-side down, on a grill pan and cook under the hot grill for 25–30 minutes, turning occasionally, until golden brown. Tip away any fat that builds up in the grill pan, as it may burn.

3 Leave the duckling to cool, then cut each half into 2 portions. Peel and core the pineapple, then cut the flesh into dice shapes. Reserve.

4 Heat the remaining oil in a large frying pan. Add the onion and garlic and fry for 3–4 minutes, until softened. Stir in the ginger, ground coriander, curry paste and sugar and stir-fry for 1 minute.

5 Stir in the coconut milk and bring to the boil. Add the duckling portions and the pineapple. Reduce the heat and simmer for 5 minutes. Sprinkle with coriander, garnish with red and green chilli flowers and serve over freshly cooked jasmine rice.

132

Rice & Noodles

With its monsoon climate and abundant rainfall, Thailand has the ideal conditions for rice growing and has become one of the major rice producers in the world. It is thought that rice grew there as far back as 3500 B.C., so it is not surprising that rice is the staple food of Thailand.

Two main varieties of rice are used in Thai cooking – long-grain and short-grain. The long-grain is Thai fragrant rice, a good quality, white, fluffy rice with delicately scented, separate grains. Glutinous or 'sticky' rice is a short-grain rice with a high starch content that causes the grains to stick together.

Noodles also play a vital part in Thai meals, and street vendors serve them as a snack at all times of the day. Rice noodles in flat ribbons (sticks) or thin vermicelli are the most common. Cellophane (mung bean) noodles are also locally made, but egg noodles are often imported from China.

crispy rice noodles

serves four

vegetable oil, for deep-frying,
      plus 1½ tbsp
200 g/7 oz rice vermicelli noodles
1 onion, finely chopped
4 garlic cloves, finely chopped
1 skinless, boneless chicken breast,
      finely chopped
2 fresh red bird's eye chillies,
      deseeded and sliced
4 tbsp dried shiitake mushrooms,
      soaked and thinly sliced
3 tbsp dried shrimp
4 spring onions, sliced
3 tbsp lime juice
2 tbsp soy sauce
2 tbsp Thai fish sauce
2 tbsp rice vinegar or white
      wine vinegar
2 tbsp soft light brown sugar
2 eggs, beaten
3 tbsp chopped fresh coriander
spring onion curls, to garnish
      (see page 212)

1 Heat the oil for deep-frying in a large frying pan or preheated wok until very hot. Add the noodles and deep-fry quickly, occasionally turning them, until puffed up, crisp and pale golden brown. Lift on to kitchen paper and drain well.

2 Heat 1 tablespoon of the remaining oil in a separate frying pan. Add the onion and garlic and fry for 1 minute. Add the chicken and stir-fry for 3 minutes. Add the chillies, mushrooms, dried shrimp and spring onions.

3 Mix the lime juice, soy sauce, fish sauce, rice vinegar and sugar together in a bowl, then stir into the frying pan and cook for a further 1 minute. Remove the frying pan from the heat.

4 Heat the remaining oil in a wide frying pan. Pour in the eggs to coat the base of the frying pan evenly, making a thin omelette. Cook until set and golden, then turn it over and cook the other side. Turn out and roll up, then slice into long ribbon strips.

5 Toss the fried noodles, stir-fried ingredients, coriander and omelette strips together. Garnish with spring onion curls and serve.

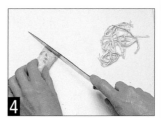

136

rice noodles with mushrooms & tofu

serves four

225 g/8 oz rice stick noodles

2 tbsp vegetable oil

1 garlic clove, finely chopped

2-cm/¾-inch piece fresh root ginger,
  finely chopped

4 shallots, thinly sliced

70 g/2½ oz shiitake
  mushrooms, sliced

100 g/3½ oz firm tofu
  (drained weight), cut into
  1.5-cm/⅝-inch dice

2 tbsp light soy sauce

1 tbsp rice wine or dry sherry

1 tbsp Thai fish sauce

1 tbsp smooth peanut butter

1 tsp chilli sauce

2 tbsp toasted peanuts, chopped

shredded fresh basil leaves

1 Place the rice stick noodles in a bowl, cover with hot water and leave to soak for 15 minutes, or according to the packet instructions. Drain well.

2 Heat the oil in a large frying pan. Add the garlic, ginger and shallots and stir-fry for 1–2 minutes, until softened and lightly browned.

3 Add the mushrooms and stir-fry for a further 2–3 minutes. Stir in the tofu and toss gently to brown lightly.

4 Mix the soy sauce, rice wine, fish sauce, peanut butter and chilli sauce together in a small bowl, then stir into the frying pan.

5 Stir in the rice noodles and toss to coat evenly in the sauce. Sprinkle with peanuts and shredded basil leaves and serve hot.

VARIATION

For an easy storecupboard dish, replace the shiitake mushrooms with canned Chinese straw mushrooms. Alternatively, use dried shiitake mushrooms, soaked and drained before use.

noodles with prawns & green peppers

serves four

250 g/9 oz rice noodles

1 tbsp vegetable oil

2 garlic cloves, crushed

1 fresh red chilli, deseeded and
    thinly sliced

1 green pepper, deseeded and
    thinly sliced

6 spring onions, roughly chopped

2 tsp cornflour

2 tbsp oyster sauce

1 tbsp Thai fish sauce

1 tsp sugar

250 ml/9 fl oz chicken stock

250 g/9 oz small cooked
    peeled prawns

2 Heat the oil in a preheated wok. Add the garlic, chilli, pepper and spring onions. Cook for 1 minute, then transfer to a plate and reserve.

3 Blend the cornflour with a little water and add to the wok with the oyster sauce, fish sauce, sugar and stock. Stir over a medium heat until the mixture boils and thickens.

4 Return the pepper and spring onion mixture to the wok with the prawns and noodles. Cook, stirring, for 2 minutes, or until heated through. Transfer to a heated serving bowl and serve immediately.

1 Prepare the noodles according to the packet instructions. Drain, rinse under cold water and drain again.

139

sesame noodles with prawns & coriander

serves four

1 garlic clove, chopped

1 spring onion, chopped

1 small fresh red chilli, deseeded
and sliced

handful of fresh coriander

300 g/10½ oz fine egg noodles

2 tbsp vegetable oil

2 tsp sesame oil

1 tsp shrimp paste

225 g/8 oz raw peeled prawns

2 tbsp lime juice

2 tbsp Thai fish sauce

1 tsp sesame seeds, toasted

COOK'S TIP

The roots of coriander are widely
used in Thai cooking, so if you
can buy fresh coriander with the
root attached, the whole plant
can be used in this dish for
maximum flavour. If not, just use
the stems and leaves.

1 Place the garlic, onion, chilli and coriander in a mortar and, using a pestle, grind to a smooth paste.

2 Drop the noodles into a saucepan of boiling water and return to the boil, then simmer for 4 minutes, or according to the packet instructions.

3 Meanwhile, heat the oils in a large frying pan or preheated wok. Stir in the shrimp paste and ground coriander mixture and stir over a medium heat for 1 minute.

4 Stir in the prawns and stir-fry for 2 minutes. Stir in the lime juice and fish sauce and cook for a further 1 minute.

5 Drain the noodles and toss them into the frying pan. Sprinkle with the toasted sesame seeds and serve immediately.

140

hot & sour noodle salad

serves four

350 g/12 oz rice vermicelli noodles

4 tbsp sesame oil

3 tbsp soy sauce

juice of 2 limes

1 tsp sugar

4 spring onions, finely sliced

1–2 tsp hot chilli sauce

2 tbsp chopped fresh coriander

1 Prepare the noodles according to the packet instructions. Drain, then toss with half the oil.

2 Mix the remaining oil, soy sauce, lime juice, sugar, spring onions and chilli sauce together in a bowl. Stir into the noodles.

3 Stir in the chopped coriander and serve immediately.

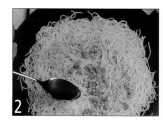

142

fried egg noodles

serves four

250 g/9 oz fine egg noodles

2 tbsp vegetable oil

2 garlic cloves, crushed

1 tbsp Thai fish sauce

3 tbsp lime juice

1 tsp sugar

2 eggs, lightly beaten

115 g/4 oz cooked peeled prawns

115 g/4 oz fresh beansprouts

6 spring onions, finely sliced

TO GARNISH

2 tbsp finely chopped
   roasted peanuts

handful of fresh coriander leaves

lime slices

1 Prepare the noodles according to the packet instructions. Drain, rinse and drain again. Reserve.

2 Heat the oil in a preheated wok. Add the garlic and cook, stirring, for 1 minute, or until lightly browned but not burnt. Stir in the fish sauce, lime juice and sugar and stir until the sugar has dissolved.

3 Quickly stir in the eggs and cook for a few seconds. Stir in the noodles to coat with the garlic and eggs. Add the prawns, beansprouts and half the spring onions.

4 When everything is heated through, transfer the mixture to a warmed serving dish. Sprinkle the remaining spring onions on top and serve, garnished with peanuts, coriander leaves and lime slices.

rice noodles with chicken & chinese leaves

serves four

200 g/7 oz rice stick noodles

1 tbsp sunflower oil

1 garlic clove, finely chopped

2-cm/¾-inch piece fresh root ginger,
    finely chopped

4 spring onions, chopped

1 fresh red bird's eye chilli,
    deseeded and sliced

300 g/10½ oz skinless, boneless
    chicken, finely chopped

2 chicken livers, finely chopped

1 celery stick, thinly sliced

1 carrot, cut into fine matchsticks

300 g/10½ oz shredded
    Chinese leaves

4 tbsp lime juice

2 tbsp Thai fish sauce

1 tbsp soy sauce

2 tbsp shredded fresh mint

slices of pickled garlic

fresh mint sprigs, to garnish

2 Heat the oil in a large frying pan or preheated wok. Add the garlic, ginger, spring onions and chilli and stir-fry for 1 minute. Stir in the chicken and chicken livers and stir-fry over a high heat for 2–3 minutes, until beginning to brown.

3 Stir in the celery and carrot and stir-fry for 2 minutes to soften. Add the Chinese leaves, then stir in the lime juice, fish sauce and soy sauce.

1 Place the rice noodles in a bowl, cover with hot water and leave to soak for 15 minutes, or according to the packet instructions. Drain well.

4 Add the noodles and stir to heat thoroughly. Sprinkle with shredded mint and pickled garlic. Serve immediately, garnished with mint sprigs.

hot & sour noodles

serves four

250 g/9 oz dried medium
    egg noodles
1 tbsp sesame oil
1 tbsp chilli oil
1 garlic clove, crushed
2 spring onions, finely chopped
55 g/2 oz button mushrooms, sliced
40 g/1½ oz dried shiitake
    mushrooms, soaked,
    drained and sliced
2 tbsp lime juice
3 tbsp light soy sauce
1 tsp sugar
TO SERVE
shredded Chinese leaves
2 tbsp shredded fresh coriander
2 tbsp toasted peanuts, chopped

1 Cook the noodles in a large saucepan of boiling water for 3–4 minutes, or according to the packet instructions. Drain well, return to the saucepan, toss with the sesame oil and reserve.

2 Heat the chilli oil in a large frying pan or preheated wok. Add the garlic, onions and button mushrooms and quickly stir-fry to soften them.

COOK'S TIP

Thai chilli oil is very hot, so if you want a milder flavour, use vegetable oil for the initial cooking instead, and add a final dribble of chilli oil just for seasoning.

3 Add the shiitake mushrooms, lime juice, soy sauce and sugar and continue stir-frying until boiling. Add the noodles and toss to mix.

4 Arrange the noodles on a bed of Chinese leaves, sprinkle with coriander and peanuts and serve.

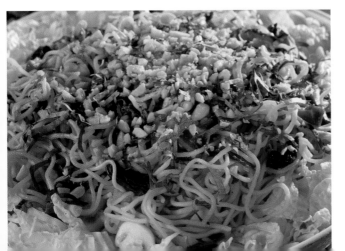

145

drunken noodles

serves four

175 g/6 oz rice stick noodles

2 tbsp vegetable oil

1 garlic clove, crushed

2 small fresh green chillies, chopped

1 small onion, thinly sliced

150 g/5 ½ oz minced lean pork
    or chicken

1 small green pepper, deseeded and
    finely chopped

4 fresh kaffir lime leaves,
    finely shredded

1 tbsp dark soy sauce

1 tbsp light soy sauce

½ tsp sugar

1 tomato, cut into thin wedges

2 tbsp finely sliced fresh
    basil leaves

1 Place the rice stick noodles in a bowl, cover with hot water and leave to soak for 15 minutes, or according to the packet instructions. Drain well.

2 Heat the oil in a large frying pan or preheated wok. Add the garlic, chillies and onion and stir-fry for 1 minute.

3 Stir in the pork and stir-fry over a high heat for a further 1 minute, then add the pepper and continue stir-frying for a further 2 minutes.

4 Stir in the lime leaves, soy sauces and sugar. Add the noodles and tomato and toss well to heat thoroughly. Sprinkle with the sliced basil leaves and serve hot.

146

pad thai noodles

serves four

250 g/9 oz rice stick noodles

3 tbsp groundnut oil

3 garlic cloves, finely chopped

125 g/4½ oz pork fillet, chopped
   into 5-mm/¼-inch pieces

200 g/7 oz cooked peeled prawns

1 tbsp sugar

3 tbsp Thai fish sauce

1 tbsp tomato ketchup

1 tbsp lime juice

2 eggs, beaten

125 g/4½ oz beansprouts

TO GARNISH

1 tsp dried red chilli flakes

2 spring onions, thickly sliced

2 tbsp chopped fresh coriander

1 Place the rice noodles in a bowl, cover with hot water and leave to soak for 15 minutes, or according to the packet instructions. Drain well and reserve until required.

2 Heat the oil in a large frying pan. Add the garlic and fry over a high heat for 30 seconds. Add the pork and stir-fry for 2–3 minutes, until browned.

3 Stir in the prawns, then add the sugar, fish sauce, ketchup and lime juice and continue stir-frying for a further 30 seconds.

4 Stir in the eggs and stir-fry until lightly set. Stir in the reserved noodles, then add the beansprouts and stir-fry for a further 30 seconds.

5 Transfer to a serving dish, sprinkle with chilli flakes, spring onions and coriander and serve.

147

thai-style noodle röstis

serves four

125 g/4½ oz rice vermicelli noodles

2 spring onions, finely shredded

1 lemon grass stalk, finely shredded

3 tbsp finely shredded fresh coconut

vegetable oil, for frying and brushing

TO FINISH

115 g/4 oz fresh beansprouts

1 small red onion, thinly sliced

1 avocado, thinly sliced

2 tbsp lime juice

2 tbsp rice wine or dry sherry

1 tsp chilli sauce

whole fresh red chillies, to garnish

1 Break the rice noodles into short pieces and place in a bowl, cover with hot water and leave to soak for 4 minutes, or according to the packet instructions. Drain thoroughly and pat dry with kitchen paper. Stir the noodles, spring onions, lemon grass and coconut together.

2 Heat a small amount of oil until very hot in a heavy-based frying pan. Brush a 9-cm/3½-inch round biscuit cutter with oil and place in the frying pan. Spoon a small amount of noodle mixture into the cutter to just cover the base of the frying pan, then press down with the back of a spoon.

3 Fry for 30 seconds, then carefully remove the cutter and continue frying the rösti until golden brown, turning it over once. Remove and drain on kitchen paper. Repeat with the remaining noodles, to make 12 röstis.

4 To finish, arrange the noodle röstis in small stacks, with beansprouts, onion and avocado between the layers. Mix the lime juice, rice wine and chilli sauce together and spoon over just before serving, garnished with whole red chillies.

rice noodles with spinach

serves four

115 g/4 oz thin rice stick noodles

2 tbsp dried shrimp (optional)

250 g/9 oz fresh young spinach
    leaves

1 tbsp groundnut oil

2 garlic cloves, finely chopped

2 tsp Thai green curry paste

1 tsp sugar

1 tbsp light soy sauce

COOK'S TIP

It is best to choose young
spinach leaves for this dish
because they are beautifully
tender and cook within a matter
of seconds. If you can only get
older spinach, however, shred
the leaves before adding to the
dish so they cook more quickly.

1 Place the noodles in a bowl,
cover with hot water and leave
to soak for 15 minutes, or according to
the packet instructions. Drain well.

2 Place the dried shrimp, if using,
in a bowl, cover with hot water
and leave to soak for 10 minutes.
Drain well. Wash the spinach
thoroughly, then drain well and
remove any tough stalks.

3 Heat the oil in a large frying pan
or preheated wok. Add the garlic
and stir-fry for 1 minute. Stir in the
curry paste and stir-fry for 30 seconds.
Stir in the reconstituted prawns,
if using, and stir-fry for 30 seconds.

4 Add the spinach and stir-fry for
1–2 minutes, or until the leaves
are just wilted.

5 Stir in the sugar and soy sauce,
then add the noodles and toss
thoroughly to mix evenly. Serve
immediately while hot.

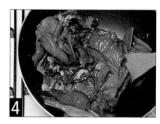

crispy duck with noodles & tamarind

serves four

3 duck breasts, total weight about
400 g/14 oz

2 garlic cloves, crushed

1½ tsp chilli paste

1 tbsp clear honey

3 tbsp dark soy sauce

½ tsp Chinese five-spice powder

250 g/9 oz rice stick noodles

1 tsp vegetable oil

1 tsp sesame oil

2 spring onions, sliced

100 g/3½ oz mangetout

2 tbsp tamarind juice

sesame seeds, for sprinkling

1 Prick the duck breast skin all over with a fork and place in a deep dish.

2 Mix the garlic, chilli paste, honey, soy sauce and five-spice powder together, then pour over the duck. Turn the breasts over to coat evenly. Cover and leave to marinate in the refrigerator for at least 1 hour.

3 Meanwhile, place the rice noodles in a bowl, cover with hot water and leave to soak for 15 minutes. Drain well.

4 Preheat the grill to high. Drain the duck breasts from the marinade, reserving it, and place on a grill rack. Cook under the hot grill for 10 minutes, turning them over occasionally, until golden brown. Remove and slice the duck breasts thinly.

5 Heat the vegetable and sesame oils in a frying pan. Add the spring onions and mangetout and toss for 2 minutes. Stir in the reserved marinade and tamarind juice and bring to the boil.

6 Add the sliced duck and noodles and toss to heat thoroughly. Serve immediately, sprinkled with sesame seeds.

152

spicy fried rice

serves four

250 g/9 oz long-grain rice

10 g/¼ oz dried mushrooms

2 tbsp vegetable oil

2 eggs, lightly beaten

2 garlic cloves, finely chopped

1 fresh red chilli, deseeded and
finely chopped

1-cm/½-inch piece fresh root ginger,
finely grated

2 tbsp soy sauce

1 tsp sugar

2 tsp Thai fish sauce

6 spring onions, finely chopped

450 g/1 lb cooked, peeled
small prawns

400 g/14 oz canned baby corn
cobs, drained and cut in half

3 tbsp chopped fresh coriander

1 Place the rice in a sieve and rinse under cold running water. Drain thoroughly. Add the rice to a large saucepan of boiling salted water, return to the boil and cook for 10 minutes, or until tender. Drain, rinse and drain again.

2 Place the mushrooms in a bowl, cover with warm water and leave to stand for 20 minutes. Drain and cut into slices.

3 Heat half the oil in a preheated wok. Add the eggs. Stir the uncooked egg to the outside edge of the wok. Cook until firm. Remove the omelette, roll up and cut into strips.

COOK'S TIP

It is important to rinse the rice under cold running water because this removes the excess starch. If you have time, wash the rice in several changes of water until the water is clear. Drain well.

4 Heat the remaining oil in the wok. Add the garlic, chilli and ginger and cook for 1 minute. Add the soy sauce, sugar, fish sauce and spring onions, stirring to dissolve the sugar. Stir in the reserved rice, prawns and corn cobs, tossing to mix. Cook for 3–4 minutes, or until the rice is heated through. Stir in the coriander, turn into a warmed serving bowl and serve.

jasmine rice with lemon & basil

serves four

400 g/14 oz jasmine rice

800 ml/28 fl oz water

finely grated rind of ½ lemon

2 tbsp shredded fresh basil

COOK'S TIP

It is important to leave the saucepan tightly covered while the rice cooks and steams inside, so the grains cook evenly and become fluffy and separate.

1 Wash the rice in several changes of cold water until the water runs clear. Bring 800 ml/28 fl oz water to the boil in a large saucepan. Add the rice.

2 Return to a rolling boil. Turn the heat to a low simmer, cover the saucepan and simmer for a further 12 minutes.

3 Remove the saucepan from the heat and leave to stand, covered, for 10 minutes.

4 Fluff up the rice with a fork, then stir in the lemon rind. Serve sprinkled with shredded basil.

egg noodle salad with lime & basil dressing

serves four

225 g/8 oz dried egg noodles

2 tsp sesame oil

1 carrot

100 g/3½ oz fresh beansprouts

½ cucumber

2 spring onions, finely shredded

150 g/5½ oz cooked turkey breast
   meat, shredded into thin slivers

chopped peanuts, for sprinkling

fresh basil leaves, to garnish

DRESSING

5 tbsp coconut milk

3 tbsp lime juice

1 tbsp light soy sauce

2 tsp Thai fish sauce

1 tsp chilli oil

1 tsp sugar

2 tbsp chopped fresh coriander

2 tbsp chopped fresh basil

1 Cook the noodles in boiling water for 4 minutes, or according to the packet instructions. Plunge them into a bowl of cold water to cool, then drain and toss in the sesame oil.

2 Use a vegetable peeler to shave off thin ribbons from the carrot. Blanch the ribbons and beansprouts in boiling water for 30 seconds, then plunge into cold water for 30 seconds. Drain well. Shave thin ribbons of cucumber with the vegetable peeler.

3 Toss the carrot, beansprouts, cucumber and spring onions together with the turkey and noodles.

4 Place all the dressing ingredients in a screw-top jar and shake well to mix evenly.

5 Add the dressing to the noodle mixture and toss. Pile on to a serving dish. Sprinkle with peanuts and garnish with basil leaves. Serve cold.

coconut rice with pineapple

serves four

200 g/7 oz long-grain rice

500 ml/18 fl oz coconut milk

2 lemon grass stalks

200 ml/7 fl oz water

2 slices fresh pineapple, peeled
and diced

2 tbsp toasted coconut

chilli sauce, to serve

VARIATION

A sweet version of this dish
can be made by simply omitting
the lemon grass and stirring in
palm sugar or caster sugar to
taste during cooking. Serve
as a dessert, with extra
pineapple slices.

1 Wash the rice in several changes of cold water until the water runs clear. Place in a large saucepan with the coconut milk.

2 Place the lemon grass on a work surface and bruise it by hitting firmly with a rolling pin or mallet. Add to the saucepan with the rice and coconut milk.

3 Add the water and bring to the boil. Reduce the heat, cover the saucepan tightly and simmer gently for 15 minutes. Remove the saucepan from the heat and fluff up the rice with a fork.

4 Remove the lemon grass and stir in the pineapple. Sprinkle with toasted coconut and serve immediately with chilli sauce.

stir-fried rice with egg strips

serves four

2 tbsp groundnut oil

1 egg, beaten with 1 tsp water

1 garlic clove, finely chopped

1 small onion, finely chopped

1 tbsp Thai red curry paste

250 g/9 oz long-grain rice, cooked

55 g/2 oz cooked peas

1 tbsp Thai fish sauce

2 tbsp tomato ketchup

2 tbsp chopped fresh coriander

TO GARNISH

fresh red chilli flowers

cucumber slices

COOK'S TIP

Many Thai rice dishes are made from leftover rice that has been cooked for an earlier meal. Nothing goes to waste and it's often stir-fried with a few simple ingredients and aromatic flavourings, as in this recipe. If you have any leftover vegetables or meat, this is a good way to use them up.

1 To make chilli flowers for the garnish, hold the stem of a fresh red chilli with your fingertips and use a small, sharp, pointed knife to cut a slit down the length from near the stem end to the tip. Turn the chilli about a quarter turn and make another cut. Repeat to make a total of 4 cuts, then scrape out the seeds. Cut each 'petal' again in half, or into quarters, to make 8–16 petals. Place the chilli flower in iced water.

2 Heat 1 teaspoon of the oil in a preheated wok or large frying pan. Pour in the egg mixture, swirling it to coat the wok evenly and make a thin layer. When set and golden, remove the egg from the wok and roll up. Reserve until required.

3 Add the remaining oil to the wok. Add the garlic and onion and stir-fry for 1 minute. Add the curry paste, then stir in the rice and peas.

4 Stir in the fish sauce, ketchup and coriander. Remove the wok from the heat and pile the rice on to a serving dish. Slice the egg roll into spiral strips, without unrolling, and use to garnish the rice. Add the cucumber slices and chilli flowers. Serve hot.

160

rice with seafood

serves four

12 live mussels in shells

2 litres/3½ pints fish stock

2 tbsp vegetable oil

1 garlic clove, crushed

1 tsp grated fresh root ginger

1 fresh red bird's eye chilli, chopped

2 spring onions, chopped

225 g/8 oz long-grain rice

2 small squid, cleaned and sliced

100 g/3½ oz firm white fish fillet,
    such as halibut or monkfish, cut
    into chunks

100 g/3½ oz raw peeled prawns

2 tbsp Thai fish sauce

3 tbsp shredded fresh coriander
    for sprinkling

1 Clean the mussels thoroughly by scrubbing or scraping the shells and pulling out any beards that are attached to them. Discard any mussels with broken shells or any that refuse to close when firmly tapped. Heat 4 tablespoons of the stock in a large saucepan. Add the mussels, cover and cook for 3–4 minutes, shaking the saucepan occasionally, until the mussels have opened. Remove the saucepan from the heat and discard any mussels that remain closed.

2 Heat the oil in a large frying pan or preheated wok. Add the garlic, ginger, chilli and spring onions and stir-fry for 30 seconds. Add the remaining stock and bring to the boil.

3 Stir in the rice, then add the squid, fish fillet and prawns. Reduce the heat and simmer gently for 15 minutes, or until the rice is cooked. Add the fish sauce and mussels.

4 Ladle into wide bowls and sprinkle with shredded coriander before serving.

VARIATION

You could use leftover cooked rice for this dish. Just simmer the seafood gently until cooked, then stir in the rice at the end.

Vegetables & Salads

Many of the vegetables, salad leaves and shoots that Thais use in cooking are native, often growing wild locally. For this reason, it can be difficult to produce truly authentic Thai salads at home.

You may have to substitute a few fresh ingredients with canned ones, but luckily you can now buy a good selection of cultivated Asian vegetables such as pak choi and Chinese leaves.

A Thai salad can make a stunning centrepiece for any dinner table. Thai cooks usually add strips of finely chopped cooked meat, fish or shellfish to their salads, or for vegetarian dishes, mushrooms or tofu are added.

Dressings are typically piquant and spicy, with the skilful balance of bitter, salt, sour, hot and sweet tastes. To finish, a sprinkling of peanuts or dried chillies, chopped coriander and a final flourish of chilli flowers add colour.

crisp pickled vegetables

serves six–eight

½ small cauliflower

½ cucumber

2 carrots

200 g/7 oz French beans

½ small Chinese cabbage

500 ml/18 fl oz rice vinegar or white
wine vinegar

1 tbsp caster sugar

1 tsp salt

3 garlic cloves

3 shallots

3 fresh red bird's eye
chillies, deseeded

5 tbsp groundnut oil

1 Trim the cauliflower. Peel and deseed the cucumber. Peel the carrots. Top and tail the beans. Trim the cabbage, then cut all the vegetables into bite-sized pieces.

2 Place the rice vinegar, sugar and salt in a large, heavy-based saucepan and bring almost to the boil. Add the vegetables, reduce the heat and simmer for 3–4 minutes, or until they are just tender, but still crisp inside. Remove the saucepan from the heat and leave the vegetables and vinegar to cool.

3 Place the garlic, shallots and chillies in a mortar and, using a pestle, grind to a smooth paste.

4 Heat the oil in a frying pan. Add the spice paste and stir-fry gently for 1–2 minutes. Add the vegetables with the vinegar and cook for a further 2 minutes to reduce the liquid slightly. Remove the frying pan from the heat and leave to cool.

5 Serve the pickles cold, or pack into jars and store in the refrigerator for up to 2 weeks.

> **COOK'S TIP**
>
> To make simple carrot 'flowers', peel the carrot thinly as usual, then use a cannelle knife or small sharp knife to cut narrow 'channels' down the length of it at regular intervals. Slice the carrot as usual and the slices will resemble flowers.

166

stir-fried green vegetables

serves four

115 g/4 oz mangetout

2 tbsp vegetable oil

3 garlic cloves, thinly sliced

2.5-cm/1-inch piece fresh root
  ginger, thinly sliced

175 g/6 oz fresh young spinach
  leaves, washed and drained

175 g/6 oz broccoli, cut into
  small florets

115 g/4 oz green beans, halved

pepper

1 tbsp Thai fish sauce

1 tbsp oyster sauce

1 tsp sugar

4 spring onions, diagonally chopped

1 Cut the mangetout in half. Heat the oil in a preheated wok. Add the garlic and ginger and cook for 1 minute. Add the spinach, broccoli and beans and cook for 2 minutes.

2 Add the mangetout to the wok and stir-fry over a high heat for 2 minutes.

3 Add pepper to taste, fish sauce, oyster sauce, sugar and spring onions. Stir-fry for a further 2 minutes.

4 Transfer to a warmed serving plate and serve.

167

spiced cashew nut curry

serves four

250 g/9 oz unsalted cashew nuts

1 tsp coriander seeds

1 tsp cumin seeds

2 cardamom pods, crushed

1 tbsp sunflower oil

1 onion, finely sliced

1 garlic clove, crushed

1 small fresh green chilli, deseeded
and chopped

1 cinnamon stick

½ tsp ground turmeric

4 tbsp coconut cream

300 ml/10 fl oz hot vegetable stock

3 dried kaffir lime leaves,
crushed

fresh coriander leaves, to garnish

freshly cooked jasmine rice, to serve

1 Place the cashew nuts in a bowl,
cover with cold water and soak
overnight. Drain thoroughly. Crush the
coriander, cumin and cardamom pods
in a mortar, using a pestle.

2 Heat the oil in a large frying pan.
Add the onion and garlic and stir-
fry for 2–3 minutes to soften, but not
brown. Add the chilli, crushed spices,
cinnamon stick and turmeric and stir-fry
for a further 1 minute.

3 Add the coconut cream and the
hot stock to the frying pan. Bring
to the boil, then add the cashew nuts
and lime leaves.

4 Cover the frying pan, reduce the
heat and simmer for 20 minutes.
Serve hot with jasmine rice garnished
with coriander leaves.

COOK'S TIP
All spices give the best flavour
when freshly crushed, but if you
prefer, you can use ready-ground
spices instead of crushing them
yourself in a mortar.

mixed vegetables in peanut sauce

serves four

2 carrots

1 small cauliflower, trimmed

2 small heads green pak choi

150 g/5½ oz French beans

2 tbsp vegetable oil

1 garlic clove, finely chopped

6 spring onions, sliced

1 tsp chilli paste

2 tbsp soy sauce

2 tbsp rice wine or dry sherry

4 tbsp smooth peanut butter

3 tbsp coconut milk

TO GARNISH

1 whole fresh red chilli

spring onion curls (see page 212)

COOK'S TIP

It's important to cut the vegetables thinly into even-sized pieces so they cook quickly and evenly. Prepare all the vegetables before you begin to cook.

1 Cut the carrots diagonally into thin slices. Cut the cauliflower into small florets, then slice the stalk thinly. Thickly slice the pak choi. Cut the beans into 3-cm/1¼-inch lengths.

2 Heat the oil in a large frying pan or preheated wok. Add the garlic and spring onions and stir-fry for 1 minute. Stir in the chilli paste and cook for a few seconds.

3 Add the carrots and cauliflower and stir-fry for 2–3 minutes.

4 Add the pak choi and beans and stir-fry for a further 2 minutes. Stir in the soy sauce and rice wine.

5 Mix the peanut butter with the coconut milk and stir into the frying pan, then cook, stirring, for a further 1 minute. Transfer to a serving dish and garnish with a red chilli and spring onion curls. Serve hot.

169

stir-fried ginger mushrooms

serves four

2 tbsp vegetable oil

3 garlic cloves, crushed

1 tbsp Thai red curry paste

½ tsp ground turmeric

425 g/15 oz canned straw
    mushrooms, drained and halved

2-cm/¾-inch piece fresh root ginger,
    finely shredded

100 ml/3½ fl oz coconut milk

40 g/1½ oz dried shiitake
    mushrooms, soaked, drained
    and sliced

1 tbsp lemon juice

1 tbsp light soy sauce

2 tsp sugar

½ tsp salt

8 cherry tomatoes, halved

200 g/7 oz firm tofu
    (drained weight), diced

fresh coriander leaves, for sprinkling

spring onion curls, to garnish
    (see page 212)

freshly cooked Thai fragrant rice,
    to serve

1 Heat the oil in a preheated wok or large frying pan. Add the garlic and fry for 1 minute, stirring. Stir in the curry paste and turmeric and cook for a further 30 seconds.

2 Stir in the straw mushrooms and ginger and stir-fry for 2 minutes. Stir in the coconut milk and bring to the boil.

3 Stir in the shiitake mushrooms, lemon juice, soy sauce, sugar and salt and heat thoroughly. Add the tomatoes and tofu and toss gently to heat through.

4 Sprinkle the coriander over the mixture and serve hot with freshly cooked fragrant rice garnished with spring onion curls.

VARIATION

You can vary the mushrooms depending on your own taste – try a mixture of oyster with the shiitake for a change. Even just ordinary cultivated button mushrooms are delicious cooked in this way.

spiced mushrooms

serves four

8 large flat mushrooms

3 tbsp sunflower oil

2 tbsp light soy sauce

1 garlic clove, crushed

2-cm/¾-inch piece fresh galangal or
    root ginger, grated

1 tbsp Thai green curry paste

8 baby corn cobs, sliced

3 spring onions, chopped

125 g/4½ oz fresh beansprouts

100 g/3½ oz firm tofu
    (drained weight), diced

2 tsp sesame seeds, toasted

TO SERVE

chopped cucumber

sliced red pepper

1 Preheat the grill to high. Remove the stalks from the mushrooms and reserve. Place the caps on a baking sheet. Mix 2 tablespoons of the oil with 1 tablespoon of the light soy sauce and brush over the mushrooms.

2 Cook the mushroom caps under the hot grill until golden and tender, turning them over once.

3 Meanwhile, chop the mushroom stalks finely. Heat the remaining oil in a large frying pan or preheated wok. Add the stalks, garlic and galangal and stir-fry for 1 minute.

4 Stir in the curry paste, baby corn cobs and spring onions and stir-fry for 1 minute. Add the beansprouts and stir for a further 1 minute.

5 Add the diced tofu and remaining soy sauce, then toss lightly to heat. Spoon the mixture into the mushroom caps.

6 Sprinkle with sesame seeds and serve with chopped cucumber and sliced red pepper.

COOK'S TIP

Galangal or ginger can be frozen for several weeks, either peeled and finely chopped ready to add to dishes, or in whole pieces. Thaw the piece or grate finely from frozen.

roasted spiced peppers

serves four

2 red peppers

2 yellow peppers

2 green peppers

2 fresh red bird's eye chillies,
    deseeded and finely chopped

1 lemon grass stalk, finely shredded

4 tbsp lime juice

2 tbsp palm sugar

1 tbsp Thai fish sauce

COOK'S TIP

The flavours will mingle best if the peppers are still slightly warm when you spoon the dressing over. Prepare the dressing while the peppers are cooking, so it's ready to pour over when they are cooked.

1 Preheat the grill or barbecue, or heat the oven to 180°C/350°F/ Gas Mark 4. Roast the peppers under the hot grill, barbecue over hot coals or roast in the oven, turning them over occasionally, until the skins are charred. Leave to cool slightly, then remove the skins. Cut each in half and remove the core and seeds.

2 Slice the peppers thickly and transfer to a large bowl.

3 Place the chillies, lemon grass, lime juice, sugar and fish sauce in a screw-top jar and shake well until thoroughly mixed.

4 Pour the dressing evenly over the peppers. Leave to cool completely, then cover with clingfilm and leave to chill in the refrigerator for at least 1 hour before serving. Transfer to a serving dish to serve.

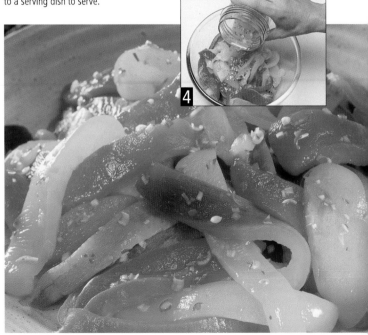

173

sweet potato cakes with soy-tomato sauce

serves four

2 sweet potatoes,
    500 g/1 lb 2 oz in total
2 garlic cloves, crushed
1 small fresh green chilli, chopped
2 fresh coriander sprigs, chopped
1 tbsp dark soy sauce
plain flour, for dusting
vegetable oil, for frying
sesame seeds, for sprinkling
fresh coriander sprigs, to garnish
SOY-TOMATO SAUCE
2 tsp vegetable oil
1 garlic clove, finely chopped
2-cm/¾-inch piece fresh root ginger,
    finely chopped
3 tomatoes, peeled and chopped
2 tbsp dark soy sauce
1 tbsp lime juice
2 tbsp chopped fresh coriander

1 To make the soy-tomato sauce, heat the oil in a preheated wok. Add the garlic and ginger and stir-fry for 1 minute. Add the tomatoes and stir-fry for a further 2 minutes. Remove the wok from the heat and stir in the soy sauce, lime juice and coriander. Keep warm.

2 Peel the sweet potatoes and grate finely (you can do this quickly in a food processor). Place the garlic, chilli and coriander in a mortar and, using a pestle, grind to a smooth paste. Stir in the soy sauce and mix with the grated sweet potatoes.

3 Spread the flour out on a plate. Divide the mixture into 12 equal portions, then dip into the flour and pat into flat, round patty shapes.

4 Heat a shallow layer of oil in a wide frying pan. Fry the sweet potato patties over a high heat until golden, turning once.

5 Drain on kitchen paper and sprinkle with sesame seeds. Transfer to a large serving plate, garnish with coriander sprigs and serve hot with the soy-tomato sauce.

174

chilli & coconut sambal

serves six–eight

1 small coconut

1 slice fresh pineapple, finely diced

1 small onion, finely chopped

2 small fresh green chillies,
   deseeded and chopped

5-cm/2-inch piece lemon
   grass, chopped

½ tsp salt

1 tsp shrimp paste

1 tbsp lime juice

2 tbsp chopped fresh coriander

fresh coriander sprigs, to garnish

VARIATION

To make a quicker version of this sambal, stir 1 teaspoon of Thai green curry paste into freshly grated coconut and add finely diced pineapple and lime juice to taste.

1 Puncture 2 of the coconut 'eyes' with a screwdriver and pour the milk out from the shell. Crack the coconut open, prise away the flesh and roughly grate it into a bowl.

2 Mix the coconut with the pineapple, onion, chillies and lemon grass.

3 Blend the salt, shrimp paste and lime juice together in a separate bowl, then stir into the sambal.

4 Stir in the coriander. Spoon into a small serving dish and garnish with fresh coriander sprigs.

176

sweet & sour potato stir-fry

serves four

4 waxy potatoes, diced

2 tbsp vegetable oil

1 yellow pepper, diced

1 red pepper, diced

1 carrot, cut into matchsticks

1 courgette, cut into matchsticks

2 garlic cloves, crushed

1 fresh red chilli, sliced

1 bunch of spring onions,
   halved lengthways

8 tbsp coconut milk

1 tsp chopped lemon grass

2 tsp lime juice

finely grated rind of 1 lime

1 tbsp chopped fresh coriander

1 Cook the diced potatoes in a saucepan of boiling water for 5 minutes. Drain thoroughly.

2 Heat the oil in a preheated wok or large frying pan. Add the potatoes, diced peppers, carrot, courgette, garlic and chilli and stir-fry for 2–3 minutes.

3 Stir in the spring onions, coconut milk, chopped lemon grass and lime juice and stir-fry for a further 5 minutes.

4 Add the lime rind and coriander and stir-fry for 1 minute. Serve hot.

COOK'S TIP

Check that the potatoes are not overcooked in step 1, otherwise the potato pieces will disintegrate when they are stir-fried in the wok.

VARIATION

Almost any combination of vegetables is suitable for this dish; the yellow and red peppers, for example, can be replaced with crisp green beans or mangetout.

potatoes in creamed coconut

serves four

600 g/1 lb 5 oz potatoes

1 onion, thinly sliced

2 fresh red bird's eye chillies,
    finely chopped

½ tsp salt

½ tsp pepper

85 g/3 oz creamed coconut

350 ml/12 fl oz vegetable or
    chicken stock

fresh coriander or basil, chopped,
    to garnish

1 Peel the potatoes then, using a sharp knife, cut them into 2-cm/¾-inch chunks.

2 Place the potatoes in a saucepan with the onion, chillies, salt, pepper and creamed coconut. Stir in the stock.

3 Bring to the boil, stirring constantly, then reduce the heat, cover and simmer gently, stirring occasionally, until the potatoes are tender.

4 Adjust the seasoning to taste if necessary, then sprinkle with chopped coriander or basil. Serve hot.

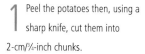

COOK'S TIP

If the potatoes are a thin-skinned, or a new variety, simply wash or scrub to remove any dirt and cook with the skins on. This adds extra nutrients to the finished dish, and cuts down on the preparation time. Baby new potatoes can be cooked whole.

178

potato & spinach yellow curry

serves four

2 garlic cloves, finely chopped

3-cm/1¼-inch piece fresh galangal, finely chopped

1 lemon grass stalk, finely chopped

1 tsp coriander seeds

3 tbsp vegetable oil

2 tsp Thai red curry paste

½ tsp ground turmeric

200 ml/7 fl oz coconut milk

250 g/9 oz potatoes, cut into 2-cm/¾-inch cubes

100 ml/3½ fl oz vegetable stock

200 g/7 oz fresh young spinach leaves

1 small onion, thinly sliced into rings

1 Place the garlic, galangal, lemon grass and coriander seeds in a mortar and, using a pestle, grind to a smooth paste.

2 Heat 2 tablespoons of the oil in a frying pan or preheated wok. Stir in the garlic paste mixture and stir-fry for 30 seconds. Stir in the curry paste and turmeric, then add the coconut milk and bring to the boil.

3 Add the potatoes and stock. Return to the boil, then reduce the heat and simmer, uncovered, for 10–12 minutes, or until the potatoes are almost tender.

4 Stir in the spinach and simmer until the leaves are wilted.

5 Meanwhile, heat the remaining oil in a separate frying pan. Add the onion and fry until crisp and golden brown.

6 Place the fried onions on top of the curry just before serving.

179

red bean curry

serves four

400 g/14 oz French beans

1 garlic clove, finely sliced

1 fresh red bird's eye chilli, deseeded and chopped

½ tsp paprika

1 piece lemon grass stalk, finely chopped

2 tsp Thai fish sauce

125 ml/4 fl oz coconut milk

1 tbsp sunflower oil

2 spring onions, sliced

VARIATION

Young runner beans can be used instead of French beans. Remove any strings from the beans, then cut at a diagonal angle in short lengths. Cook as in the recipe until tender.

1 Cut the beans into 5-cm/2-inch pieces and cook in boiling water for 2 minutes. Drain well.

2 Place the garlic, chilli, paprika, lemon grass, Thai fish sauce and coconut milk in a blender or food processor and process to a smooth paste.

3 Heat the oil in a large frying pan or preheated wok. Add the spring onions and stir-fry over a high heat for 1 minute. Add the paste and bring the mixture to the boil.

4 Simmer for 3–4 minutes to reduce the liquid by about half. Add the beans and simmer for a further 1–2 minutes, or until tender. Transfer to a serving dish and serve hot.

vegetable & coconut curry

serves four

1 kg/2 lb 4 oz mixed vegetables

1 onion, roughly chopped

3 garlic cloves, thinly sliced

2.5-cm/1-inch piece fresh root
ginger, thinly sliced

2 fresh green chillies, deseeded
and finely chopped

1 tbsp vegetable oil

1 tsp ground turmeric

1 tsp ground coriander

1 tsp ground cumin

200 g/7 oz creamed coconut

600 ml/1 pint boiling water

salt and pepper

2 tbsp chopped fresh coriander,
to garnish

freshly cooked rice, to serve

1 Cut the mixed vegetables into chunks. Place the onion, garlic, ginger and chillies in a food processor and process until almost smooth.

2 Heat the oil in a large, heavy-based frying pan. Add the onion mixture and cook for 5 minutes.

3 Add the turmeric, coriander and cumin and cook for 3–4 minutes, stirring. Add the mixed vegetables and stir to coat in the spice paste.

4 Mix the creamed coconut and boiling water together in a jug. Stir until the coconut has dissolved. Add the coconut milk to the vegetables, cover and simmer for 30–40 minutes, or until the vegetables are tender.

5 Season to taste with salt and pepper, garnish with the chopped coriander and serve with rice.

COOK'S TIP

Use whatever vegetables you
have to hand, such as
cauliflower, courgettes, potatoes,
carrots and green beans.

182

asian vegetables with yellow bean sauce

serves four

1 aubergine

salt

2 tbsp vegetable oil

3 garlic cloves, crushed

4 spring onions, chopped

1 small red pepper, deseeded and
 thinly sliced

4 baby corn cobs, halved
 lengthways

85 g/3 oz mangetout

200 g/7 oz green pak choi,
 roughly shredded

425 g/14½ oz canned Chinese
 straw mushrooms, drained

125 g/4½ oz fresh beansprouts

2 tbsp rice wine or dry sherry

2 tbsp yellow bean sauce

2 tbsp dark soy sauce

1 tsp chilli sauce

1 tsp sugar

125 ml/4 fl oz chicken or
 vegetable stock

1 tsp cornflour

2 tsp water

1 Cut the aubergine into 5-cm/2-inch long matchsticks. Place in a colander, sprinkle with salt and leave to stand for 30 minutes. Rinse in cold water and dry with kitchen paper.

2 Heat the oil in a frying pan or preheated wok. Add the garlic, spring onions and pepper and stir-fry over a high heat for 1 minute. Stir in the aubergine pieces and stir-fry for a further 1 minute, or until softened.

3 Stir in the corn cobs and mangetout and stir-fry for 1 minute. Add the pak choi, mushrooms and beansprouts and stir-fry for 30 seconds.

4 Mix the rice wine, yellow bean sauce, soy sauce, chilli sauce and sugar together in a bowl, then add to the frying pan with the stock. Bring to the boil, stirring constantly.

5 Slowly blend the cornflour with the water to form a smooth paste, then stir quickly into the frying pan and cook for a further 1 minute. Serve immediately.

crispy tofu with chilli-soy sauce

serves four

300 g/10½ oz firm tofu
  (drained weight)
2 tbsp vegetable oil
1 garlic clove, sliced
1 carrot, cut into matchsticks
½ green pepper, deseeded and cut
  into matchsticks
1 fresh red bird's eye chilli,
  deseeded and finely chopped
2 tbsp soy sauce
1 tbsp lime juice
1 tbsp Thai fish sauce
1 tbsp soft light brown sugar
pickled garlic slices, to serve
  (optional)

1 Drain the tofu and pat dry with kitchen paper. Cut the tofu into 2-cm/¾-inch cubes.

2 Heat the oil in a preheated wok or large frying pan. Add the garlic and stir-fry for 1 minute. Remove the garlic and add the tofu, then fry quickly, turning gently to brown well on all sides.

3 Remove the tofu, drain well and keep hot. Stir the carrot and pepper into the wok and stir-fry for 1 minute.

4 Transfer the carrot and pepper to a dish and pile the tofu on top.

5 Mix the chilli, soy sauce, lime juice, fish sauce and sugar together in a bowl, stirring until the sugar is dissolved.

6 Spoon the sauce over the tofu and serve topped with pickled garlic slices, if using. Serve hot.

stir-fried broccoli in oyster sauce

serves four

400 g/14 oz broccoli

1 tbsp groundnut oil

2 shallots, finely chopped

1 garlic clove, finely chopped

1 tbsp rice wine or dry sherry

5 tbsp oyster sauce

$\frac{1}{4}$ tsp pepper

1 tsp chilli oil

1 Cut the broccoli into small florets. Blanch in a saucepan of boiling water for 30 seconds, then drain well.

2 Heat the oil in a large frying pan or preheated wok. Add the shallots and garlic and stir-fry for 1–2 minutes, or until golden brown.

3 Stir in the broccoli and stir-fry for 2 minutes. Add the rice wine and oyster sauce and stir for a further 1 minute.

4 Stir in the pepper and drizzle with a little chilli oil just before serving.

COOK'S TIP

To make chilli oil, put fresh red or green chillies into a jar and top up with olive oil or a light vegetable oil. Cover with a lid and leave to infuse for at least 3 weeks before using.

187

vegetable fritters with sweet chilli dip

serves four

150 g/5½ oz plain flour

1 tsp ground coriander

1 tsp ground cumin

1 tsp ground turmeric

1 tsp salt

½ tsp pepper

2 garlic cloves, finely chopped

3-cm/1¼-inch piece fresh root
    ginger, chopped

2 small fresh green chillies,
    finely chopped

1 tbsp chopped fresh coriander

about 225 ml/8 fl oz cold water

1 onion, chopped

1 potato, roughly grated

85 g/3 oz canned sweetcorn kernels

1 small aubergine, diced

125 g/4½ oz Chinese broccoli, cut
    into short lengths

coconut oil, for deep-frying

SWEET CHILLI DIP

2 fresh red bird's eye chillies,
    finely chopped

4 tbsp caster sugar

4 tbsp rice vinegar or white
    wine vinegar

1 tbsp light soy sauce

1 Make the dip by mixing all the ingredients together thoroughly until the sugar is dissolved. Cover and reserve until required.

2 To make the fritters, place the flour in a bowl and stir in the coriander, cumin, turmeric, salt and pepper. Add the garlic, ginger, green chillies and coriander with just enough cold water to form a thick batter.

3 Add the onion, potato, sweetcorn, aubergine and broccoli to the batter and stir well to distribute the ingredients evenly.

4 Heat the oil in a deep frying pan or wok to 180–190°C/ 350–375°F, or until a cube of bread browns in 30 seconds. Drop tablespoons of the batter into the hot oil and fry in batches until golden and crisp, turning once.

5 Drain the fritters well on kitchen paper and serve hot with the sweet chilli dip.

188

sweetcorn fritters

serves four

55 g/2 oz plain flour

1 large egg

2 tsp Thai green curry paste

5 tbsp coconut milk

400 g/14 oz canned or frozen
    sweetcorn kernels

4 spring onions

1 tbsp chopped fresh coriander

1 tbsp chopped fresh basil

salt and pepper

vegetable oil, for shallow frying

lime wedges, to garnish

chilli relish, to serve

1 Place the flour, egg, curry paste, coconut milk and about half the sweetcorn kernels in a food processor and process to a smooth, thick batter.

2 Finely chop the spring onions and stir into the batter with the remaining sweetcorn, chopped coriander and basil. Season well with salt and pepper.

3 Heat a small amount of oil in a wide, heavy-based frying pan. Drop in tablespoonfuls of the batter and cook for 2–3 minutes, or until golden brown.

4 Turn them over and cook for a further 2–3 minutes, until golden. Fry in batches, making 12–16 fritters, keeping the cooked fritters hot while you cook the remaining batter.

5 Transfer the fritters to a serving plate, garnish with lime wedges and serve with a chilli relish.

190

pak choi with crabmeat

serves four

2 heads green pak choi, about
    250 g/9 oz in total
2 tbsp vegetable oil
1 garlic clove, thinly sliced
2 tbsp oyster sauce
100 g/3½ oz cherry
    tomatoes, halved
175 g/6 oz canned white
    crabmeat, drained
salt and pepper

VARIATION
For a vegetarian version of this dish, omit the crabmeat and replace the oyster sauce with 2 tablespoons of light soy sauce.

1 Using a sharp knife, cut the pak choi into 2.5-cm/1-inch thick slices.

2 Heat the oil in a large frying pan or preheated wok. Add the garlic and stir-fry quickly over a high heat for 1 minute.

3 Add the pak choi and stir-fry for 2–3 minutes, until the leaves wilt but the stalks are still crisp.

4 Add the oyster sauce and tomatoes and stir-fry for a further 1 minute.

5 Add the crabmeat and season well with salt and pepper. Stir to heat thoroughly and break up the crabmeat before serving.

191

bamboo shoot salad

serves four

2 shallots

2 garlic cloves

2 tbsp Thai fish sauce

3 tbsp lime juice

½ tsp dried chilli flakes

1 tsp granulated sugar

1 tbsp short-grain rice

2 tsp sesame seeds

350 g/12 oz canned bamboo
    shoots, drained

2 spring onions, chopped

Chinese leaves or lettuce, shredded

fresh mint leaves, to garnish

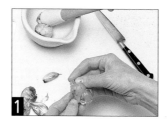

1 Preheat the grill to medium. Place the shallots and garlic, unpeeled, under the hot grill and cook until charred on the outside and tender inside. Leave to cool slightly, then remove the skins and discard. Place the flesh in a mortar and grind to a smooth paste with the pestle.

2 Mix the shallot and garlic paste with the fish sauce, lime juice, chilli flakes and sugar in a small bowl.

3 Place the rice and sesame seeds in a heavy-based frying pan and cook to a rich golden brown colour, shaking the frying pan to brown evenly. Remove the frying pan from the heat and leave to cool slightly. Crush the toasted rice and sesame seeds lightly in a mortar, using a pestle.

4 Use a sharp knife to shred the bamboo shoots into fine matchsticks and place in a bowl. Stir in the shallot and garlic dressing, tossing well to coat evenly. Stir in the toasted rice and sesame seeds, then the spring onions.

5 Pile the salad on to a serving dish and surround with shredded Chinese leaves. Garnish with mint leaves and serve.

192

asian lettuce cups

serves four

8 leaves cos lettuce, or similar firm
    lettuce leaves

2 carrots

2 celery sticks

100 g/3½ oz baby corn cobs

2 spring onions

100 g/3½ oz fresh beansprouts

2 tbsp roasted peanuts, chopped

DRESSING

2 tbsp smooth peanut butter

3 tbsp lime juice

3 tbsp coconut milk

2 tsp Thai fish sauce

1 tsp caster sugar

1 tsp grated fresh root ginger

¼ tsp Thai red curry paste

1 Wash and trim the lettuce leaves, leaving them whole. Arrange on a serving plate or on individual plates.

2 Trim the carrots and celery and cut into fine matchsticks. Trim the corn cobs and onions and slice both diagonally.

3 Toss all the prepared vegetables together with the beansprouts. Divide the salad mixture evenly between the individual lettuce cups.

COOK'S TIP

Choose leaves with a deep cup shape to hold the salad neatly. If you prefer, Chinese leaves may be used in place of the cos lettuce. To remove the leaves from the whole head without tearing them, cut a thick slice from the base end so the leaves are not attached by their stems, then gently ease away the leafy parts.

4 To make the dressing, place all the ingredients in a screw-top jar and shake well until thoroughly mixed.

5 Spoon the dressing evenly over the salad cups and sprinkle with chopped peanuts. Serve immediately.

aubergine & mushroom stuffed omelette

serves four

3 tbsp vegetable oil

1 garlic clove, finely chopped

1 small onion, finely chopped

1 small aubergine, diced

½ small green pepper, deseeded
    and chopped

1 large dried shiitake mushroom,
    soaked, drained and sliced

1 tomato, diced

1 tbsp light soy sauce

½ tsp sugar

¼ tsp pepper

2 large eggs

dipping sauce, to serve

TO GARNISH

salad leaves

tomato wedges

cucumber slices

COOK'S TIP

If you heat the frying pan
thoroughly before adding
the oil, and heat the oil before
adding the ingredients, you
should not have a problem
with the ingredients sticking
to the frying pan.

1 Heat half the oil in a large frying pan. Add the garlic and fry over a high heat for 30 seconds. Add the onion and the aubergine and continue to stir-fry until golden.

2 Add the green pepper and stir-fry for a further 1 minute to soften. Stir in the mushroom, tomato, soy sauce, sugar and pepper. Remove from the frying pan and keep hot.

3 Beat the eggs together lightly. Heat the remaining oil in a clean frying pan, swirling to coat a wide area. Pour in the egg and swirl to set around the frying pan.

4 When the egg is set, spoon the filling into the centre. Fold in the sides of the omelette to form a square parcel.

5 Slide the omelette carefully on to a warmed dish and garnish with salad leaves, tomato wedges and cucumber slices. Serve with a dipping sauce.

thai green salad

serves four

1 small head cos lettuce

1 bunch of spring onions

½ cucumber

4 tbsp coarsely shredded and
   toasted fresh coconut

DRESSING

4 tbsp lime juice

2 tbsp Thai fish sauce

1 small fresh red bird's eye chilli,
   finely chopped

1 tsp sugar

1 garlic clove, crushed

2 tbsp chopped fresh coriander

1 tbsp chopped fresh mint

COOK'S TIP

This salad is good for picnics –
to pack it easily, pack the leaves
into a large polythene container
or unbreakable salad bowl, and
nestle the jar of dressing in the
centre. Cover with clingfilm.
Packed this way, the salad stays
crisp and if the dressing leaks
during transit, there's no mess.

1 Tear or roughly shred the lettuce leaves and place in a large salad bowl.

2 Trim and thinly slice the spring onions diagonally, then add them to the salad bowl.

3 Use a vegetable peeler to shave thin slices along the length of the cucumber and add to the salad bowl.

4 Place all the ingredients for the dressing in a screw-top jar and shake well to mix thoroughly.

5 Pour the dressing over the salad and toss well to coat all the leaves evenly.

6 Sprinkle the coconut over the salad and toss in lightly just before serving.

196

cucumber salad

serves four

1 cucumber

1 tsp salt

1 small red onion

1 garlic clove, crushed

½ tsp chilli paste

2 tsp Thai fish sauce

1 tbsp lime juice

1 tsp sesame oil

COOK'S TIP

Once the salad is made, it can be chilled with the dressing for 1–2 hours, but is best eaten on the day of making.

VARIATION

For a change, peel the cucumber and cut it into small dice, then salt and drain as above. Drain and toss with the onions and dressing as before.

1 Trim the cucumber and coarsely grate the flesh. Place in a sieve over a large bowl, sprinkle with the salt and leave to stand for 20 minutes. Discard the liquid.

2 Chop the onion finely, then toss into the cucumber. Spoon into 4 serving bowls. Alternatively, use a large serving dish.

3 Mix the garlic, chilli paste, fish sauce, lime juice and sesame oil together in a small bowl, then spoon over the salad. Cover with clingfilm and leave to chill in the refrigerator before serving.

198

thai-style caesar salad

serves four

1 large head cos lettuce, with outer
leaves removed, or 2 hearts
vegetable oil, for deep-frying
4–6 large rice paper wrappers or
115 g/4 oz rice paper flakes
small bunch of fresh coriander,
leaves stripped from stems
DRESSING
80 ml/3 fl oz rice vinegar
2–3 tbsp Thai fish sauce
2 garlic cloves, roughly chopped
1 tbsp sugar
2.5-cm/1-inch piece fresh root
ginger, roughly chopped
125 ml/4 fl oz sunflower oil
salt and pepper

1 Tear the lettuce into bite-sized pieces and place in a salad bowl.

2 To make the dressing, place the vinegar, fish sauce, garlic, sugar and ginger in a food processor and process for 15–30 seconds.

3 With the motor running, gradually pour in the sunflower oil until a creamy liquid forms. Season to taste with salt and pepper and pour into a jug. Reserve.

4 Heat about 7.5 cm/3 inches of vegetable oil in a deep-fat fryer or wok to 180–190°C/350–375°F, or until a cube of bread browns in 30 seconds.

5 Meanwhile, break the rice wrappers into bite-sized pieces and dip each into a bowl of water to soften. Lay on a clean tea towel and pat completely dry.

6 Working in batches, add the rice paper pieces to the hot oil and deep-fry for 15 seconds, or until crisp. Using a slotted spoon, transfer to kitchen paper to drain.

7 Add the coriander leaves to the lettuce and toss to mix. Add the fried rice paper 'crisps' and drizzle over the dressing. Toss to coat the leaves and serve immediately.

VARIATION
Substitute 2 tablespoons of the sunflower oil with sesame oil for a different flavour.

199

green pawpaw salad

serves four

225 g/8 oz mangetout

2 pawpaws

DRESSING

2 garlic cloves, crushed

2 fresh red chillies, deseeded and
finely chopped

1 tsp sugar

2 tbsp soy sauce

juice of 1 lime

½ head of Chinese leaves

TO GARNISH

12 cherry tomatoes

2 tbsp chopped peanuts

VARIATION

Replace the chopped peanuts
with chopped cashew nuts, if
you prefer. For an extra touch,
lightly toast the nuts before
adding to the salad.

1 Place the mangetout in a
saucepan of boiling salted water.
Return to the boil and cook for
2 minutes. Drain through a sieve, then
refresh under cold water. Cut into thin
matchsticks and place in a bowl.

2 Peel the pawpaws, remove the
black seeds and chop the flesh
into the bowl with the mangetout.
Cover and chill in the refrigerator until
ready to serve.

3 Mix the garlic, chillies, sugar, soy
sauce and lime juice together in a
bowl. Pour over the pawpaw salad and
mix well.

4 Arrange the Chinese leaves in a
large serving bowl, then place the
salad on top. Cut the cherry tomatoes
in half. Garnish the salad with
the tomatoes and chopped peanuts
before serving.

pineapple & cucumber salad

serves four

1 cucumber

1 small fresh pineapple

1 red onion, thinly sliced

1 bunch of watercress

DRESSING

3 tbsp lemon juice

2 tbsp soy sauce

1 tsp sugar

1 tsp chilli sauce

2 tbsp chopped fresh mint

1 Peel the cucumber and cut into quarters lengthways. Scoop out the seeds with a teaspoon and cut each quarter into 1-cm/½-inch pieces. Place in a bowl.

2 Peel the pineapple and cut into quarters lengthways. Remove the core. Cut each quarter in half lengthways, then cut into 1-cm/½-inch pieces and add to the cucumber. Add the onion and watercress and mix.

3 To make the dressing, place all the ingredients in a small bowl and whisk together.

4 Pour the dressing over the salad and toss together. Transfer to a large serving platter and serve.

202

thai salad with peanut dressing

serves four

250 g/9 oz white cabbage,
   shredded

4 carrots, cut into matchsticks

4 celery sticks, cut into matchsticks

250 g/9 oz beansprouts

½ cucumber, cut into matchsticks

PEANUT SAUCE

2 tbsp smooth peanut butter

200 ml/7 fl oz coconut cream

2 tsp Thai red curry paste

1 tbsp Thai fish sauce

1 tbsp soft light brown sugar

TO GARNISH

fried onions

sliced fresh green chilli

1 Set a steamer above a saucepan of boiling water. Add the cabbage, carrots and celery and steam for 3–4 minutes until just tender. Leave to cool.

2 Arrange the beansprouts on a large, shallow serving dish. Arrange the cabbage, carrots, celery and cucumber on top.

3 To make the sauce, place all the ingredients in a saucepan. Heat gently, stirring, adding a little hot water, if necessary, to make a coating sauce.

4 Spoon a little of the sauce over the vegetables and garnish with fried onions and sliced chilli. Serve the rest of the sauce separately.

203

grilled aubergine & sesame salad

serves four

8 baby aubergines

salt

2 tsp chilli oil

1 tbsp soy sauce

1 tbsp Thai fish sauce

1 tbsp sunflower oil

1 garlic clove, thinly sliced

1 fresh red bird's eye chilli,
   deseeded and sliced

1 tsp sesame oil

1 tbsp lime juice

1 tsp soft light brown sugar

1 tbsp chopped fresh mint

1 tbsp sesame seeds, toasted

fresh mint leaves, to garnish

1 Cut the aubergines lengthways into thin slices to within 2.5 cm/ 1 inch of the stem end. Place in a colander, sprinkling with salt between the slices, and leave to stand for 30 minutes. Rinse in cold water and pat dry with kitchen paper.

2 Preheat the grill to medium. Mix the chilli oil, soy sauce and fish sauce together in a bowl, then brush over the aubergines. Cook under the hot grill, or barbecue over hot coals,

for 6–8 minutes, turning them over occasionally and brushing with more chilli oil glaze, until golden brown and softened. Arrange on a serving platter.

3 Heat the sunflower oil in a large frying pan. Add the garlic and chilli and fry for 1–2 minutes, until just beginning to brown. Remove the frying pan from the heat and add the sesame oil, lime juice, brown sugar and any remaining chilli oil glaze.

4 Add the chopped mint and spoon the warm dressing over the aubergines. Leave to marinate for 20 minutes, then sprinkle with the toasted sesame seeds. Serve garnished with mint leaves.

carrot & mango salad

serves four

4 carrots

1 small ripe mango

200 g/7 oz firm tofu
(drained weight)

1 tbsp snipped fresh chives

DRESSING

2 tbsp orange juice

1 tbsp lime juice

1 tsp clear honey

½ tsp orange flower water

1 tsp sesame oil

1 tsp sesame seeds, toasted

1 Coarsely grate the carrots. Peel, stone and thinly slice the mango.

2 Cut the tofu into 1-cm/½-inch dice and toss together with the carrots and mango in a wide salad bowl.

3 To make the dressing, place all the ingredients in a screw-top jar and shake well until thoroughly mixed. Pour the dressing over the salad and toss well to coat the salad evenly.

4 Just before serving, toss the salad lightly and sprinkle with snipped chives. Serve immediately.

COOK'S TIP

A food processor will grate the carrots in seconds — especially useful if you're catering for a crowd.

thai seafood salad

serves four

450 g/1 lb live mussels in shells
8 raw tiger prawns
350 g/12 oz squid, cleaned and
  sliced widthways into rings
115 g/4 oz cooked peeled prawns
1 red onion, finely sliced
1 red pepper, deseeded and
  finely sliced
115 g/4 oz beansprouts
115 g/4 oz shredded pak choi
DRESSING
1 garlic clove, crushed
1 tsp grated fresh root ginger
1 fresh red chilli, deseeded and
  finely chopped
2 tbsp chopped fresh coriander
1 tbsp lime juice
1 tsp finely grated lime rind
1 tbsp light soy sauce
5 tbsp sunflower or groundnut oil
2 tsp sesame oil
salt and pepper
4 tbsp cold water

1 Clean the mussels by scrubbing or scraping the shells and pulling out any beards that are attached. Discard any with broken shells or any that refuse to close when tapped.

2 Place the mussels in a saucepan with just the water that clings to their shells. Cook over a high heat for 3–4 minutes, shaking the saucepan occasionally, until the mussels have opened. Discard any that remain closed. Sieve the mussels, reserving the cooking liquid, and refresh under cold water. Drain again and reserve.

3 Bring the reserved cooking liquid to the boil and add the tiger prawns. Simmer for 5 minutes. Add the squid and cook for a further 2 minutes until the prawns and squid are cooked through. Remove with a slotted spoon and plunge immediately into a bowl of cold water. Reserve the cooking liquid. Drain the prawns and squid.

4 Remove the mussels from their shells and place in a bowl with the tiger prawns, squid and cooked peeled prawns. Leave to chill in the refrigerator for 1 hour.

5 To make the dressing, place all the ingredients, except the oils, in a blender or food processor and process to a smooth paste. Add the oils, reserved cooking liquid, salt and pepper to taste, then the cold water. Process again to mix.

6 Just before serving, mix the onion, red pepper, beansprouts and pak choi in a bowl and toss with 2–3 tablespoons of the dressing. Arrange the vegetables on a large serving plate or in a bowl. Toss the remaining dressing with the seafood to coat and add to the vegetables. Serve immediately.

206

thai noodle salad with prawns

serves four

85 g/3 oz rice vermicelli noodles or
rice sticks

175 g/6 oz mangetout, cut
crossways in half, if large

5 tbsp lime juice

4 tbsp Thai fish sauce

1 tbsp sugar, or to taste

2.5-cm/1-inch piece fresh root
ginger, finely chopped

1 fresh red chilli, deseeded and
thinly sliced on the diagonal

4 tbsp chopped fresh coriander, plus
extra for garnishing

10-cm/4-inch piece cucumber,
peeled, deseeded and diced

2 spring onions, thinly sliced
on the diagonal

16–20 large cooked peeled prawns

2 tbsp chopped unsalted peanuts or
cashews (optional)

TO GARNISH

4 cooked whole prawns

lemon slices

VARIATION

Replace the fresh coriander with
the same amount of mint and the
lemon slices with lime.

---

1 Place the rice noodles in a large
bowl and pour over enough hot
water to cover. Leave to stand for
4 minutes, until soft. Drain and rinse
under cold running water, then drain
again and reserve.

2 Bring a saucepan of water to the
boil. Add the mangetout and
simmer for 1 minute. Drain, rinse under
cold running water until cold, then
drain and reserve.

3 Whisk the lime juice, fish sauce,
sugar, ginger, chilli and coriander
together in a large bowl. Stir in the
cucumber and spring onions. Add the
drained noodles, mangetout and the
prawns. Toss the salad gently together.

4 Divide the noodle salad between
4 large plates. Sprinkle with
chopped coriander and the peanuts,
if using, then garnish each plate with
a whole prawn and a lemon slice.
Serve immediately.

COOK'S TIP

There are many sizes of rice
noodles available – make sure
you use the thin rice noodles,
called rice vermicelli, rice sticks
or *sen mee*, otherwise the salad
will be too heavy.

208

grilled beef salad

serves four

50 g/1¾ oz dried oyster mushrooms

600 g/1 lb 5 oz rump steak

1 red pepper, deseeded and
thinly sliced

40 g/1½ oz roasted cashew nuts

red and green lettuce leaves

fresh mint leaves, to garnish

DRESSING

2 tbsp sesame oil

2 tbsp Thai fish sauce

2 tbsp sweet sherry

2 tbsp oyster sauce

1 tbsp lime juice

1 fresh red chilli, deseeded and
finely chopped

1 Place the mushrooms in a heatproof bowl, cover with boiling water and leave to stand for 20 minutes. Drain, then cut into slices.

2 Preheat the grill or griddle pan to medium. To make the dressing, place all the ingredients in a bowl and whisk to combine.

3 Cook the steak under the hot grill, or in a griddle pan, turning once, for 5 minutes, or until browned on both sides and rare in the middle. Cook for longer if desired.

4 Slice the steak into thin strips and place in a bowl with the mushrooms, pepper and nuts. Add the dressing and toss together.

5 Arrange the lettuce on a large serving platter and place the beef mixture on top. Garnish with mint leaves. Serve at room temperature.

hot & sour beef salad

serves four

1 tsp black peppercorns

1 tsp coriander seeds

1 dried red bird's eye chilli

¼ tsp Chinese five-spice powder

250 g/9 oz lean beef fillet

1 tbsp dark soy sauce

6 spring onions

1 carrot

¼ cucumber

8 radishes

1 red onion

¼ head Chinese leaves

2 tbsp groundnut oil

1 garlic clove, crushed

1 tsp finely chopped lemon grass

1 tbsp chopped fresh mint

1 tbsp chopped fresh coriander

DRESSING

3 tbsp lime juice

1 tbsp light soy sauce

2 tsp soft light brown sugar

1 tsp sesame oil

1 Crush the peppercorns, coriander seeds and chilli in a mortar using a pestle, then mix with the five-spice powder and sprinkle on a plate. Brush the beef all over with soy sauce, then roll it in the spices to coat evenly.

2 Cut the spring onions into 6-cm/2½-inch lengths, then shred them finely lengthways. Place in a bowl of iced water and leave until curled. Drain well.

3 Cut the carrot into very thin diagonal slices. Halve the cucumber lengthways and scoop out the seeds, then slice thinly. Cut the radishes into flower shapes.

4 Slice the onion thinly, cutting each slice from top to root. Roughly shred the Chinese leaves. Toss all the vegetables, except the spring onion curls, together in a large salad bowl.

5 Heat the groundnut oil in a large, heavy-based frying pan. Add the garlic and lemon grass and fry until just turning golden brown. Add the beef and press down with a spatula to ensure it browns evenly. Cook for 3–4 minutes, turning it over once, depending on the thickness. Remove the frying pan from the heat.

6 Slice the beef thinly and toss into the salad with the mint and coriander. Mix all the dressing ingredients together in a bowl and stir into the frying pan, then spoon over the salad. Garnish with the spring onion curls and serve.

roast duck salad

serves four

2 duck breasts

2 Little Gem lettuces, shredded

115 g/4 oz beansprouts

1 yellow pepper, deseeded and cut
    into thin strips

½ cucumber, deseeded and cut
    into matchsticks

DRESSING

juice of 2 limes

3 tbsp Thai fish sauce

1 tbsp soft brown sugar

2 tsp sweet chilli sauce

2.5-cm/1-inch piece fresh root
    ginger, finely grated

3 tbsp chopped fresh mint

3 tbsp chopped fresh basil

TO GARNISH

2 tsp shredded lime rind

2 tbsp shredded coconut, toasted

1 Preheat the oven to 200°C/ 400°F/Gas Mark 6. Place the duck breasts on a rack set over a roasting tin and roast in the oven for 20–30 minutes, or until cooked as desired and the skin is crisp. Remove from the oven and leave to cool.

2 Mix the lettuce, beansprouts, pepper and cucumber together in a large bowl. Cut the cooled duck into strips and add to the salad. Mix well.

3 To make the dressing, whisk all the ingredients together in a separate bowl. Add the dressing to the salad and toss well.

4 Turn the salad out on to a serving plate and garnish with lime rind and shredded coconut before serving.

Desserts & Drinks

The normal conclusion to a Thai meal is a basket of fruit, often including mangoes, mangosteens, jackfruit, guavas and lychees. Desserts and sweetmeats are mostly made at home for between-meal treats, or made by experts for special occasions, because their preparation can be time-consuming and often requires skilful blending and shaping.

Rice, usually of the glutinous variety, and tapioca are both key ingredients in many sweets and cakes, often moulded or coloured, soaked in scented syrups.

Many Thai drinks are colourful and exotic in flavour. They use the abundant fruits and coconut milk in long, refreshing drinks, sweetened with palm sugar and often served with a dash of whisky or other spirit.

thai rice pudding

serves four

100 g/3½ oz short-grain rice

2 tbsp palm sugar

1 cardamom pod, split

300 ml/10 fl oz coconut milk

150 ml/5 fl oz water

3 eggs

200 ml/7 fl oz coconut cream

1½ tbsp caster sugar

sweetened coconut flakes,
   to decorate

fresh fruit, to serve

COOK'S TIP

Cardamom is quite a powerful
spice, so if you find it too strong
it can be left out, or replaced
with a little ground cinnamon.

1 Preheat the oven to 180°C/350°F/
Gas Mark 4. Place the rice and
palm sugar in a saucepan. Crush the
seeds from the cardamom pod in a
mortar using a pestle and add to the
saucepan. Stir in the coconut milk
and water.

2 Bring to the boil, stirring to
dissolve the sugar. Reduce the
heat and leave to simmer, uncovered,
stirring occasionally, for 20 minutes,
until the rice is tender and most of the
liquid is absorbed.

3 Spoon the rice into 4 individual
ovenproof dishes and spread
evenly. Place the dishes in a wide
roasting tin and pour in enough water
to come halfway up the sides.

4 Beat the eggs, coconut cream and
caster sugar together in a bowl,
then spoon over the rice. Cover with
foil and bake in the preheated oven for
45–50 minutes, until the custard sets.

5 Turn out the puddings and
decorate with coconut flakes.
Serve warm or cold with fresh fruit.

strings of gold

serves four

7 egg yolks

1 tbsp egg white

500 g/1 lb 2 oz granulated sugar

200 ml/7 fl oz water

handful of fresh scented
    jasmine flowers

TO DECORATE

pomegranate seeds

sliced kiwi fruit

sliced apple

1 Press the egg yolks and egg white through a fine sieve into a bowl, then whisk lightly.

2 Place the sugar and water in a large saucepan and heat gently until the sugar dissolves. Add the jasmine flowers, bring to the boil and boil rapidly until a thin syrup forms. Remove the jasmine flowers with a slotted spoon and discard.

3 Bring the syrup to simmering point. Using a piping bag with a fine nozzle, quickly drizzle the egg mixture into the syrup in a thin stream to form loose nests or pyramid shapes.

4 As soon as the threads set, remove the nests carefully and drain well on kitchen paper. Arrange in a warmed serving dish and decorate with the pomegranate seeds, kiwi fruit and apple. Serve immediately.

VARIATION
If you can't get hold of fresh scented jasmine flowers, add a few drops of rosewater or orange flower water to the syrup instead.

mangoes in lemon grass syrup

serves four

2 large ripe mangoes

1 lime

1 lemon grass stalk, chopped

3 tbsp caster sugar

COOK'S TIP

To serve this dessert on a hot day, particularly if it is to stand for a while, place the dish on a bed of crushed ice to keep the fruit and syrup chilled.

1 Halve the mangoes, remove the stones and peel off the skins.

2 Slice the flesh into long, thin slices and carefully arrange them in a wide serving dish.

3 Remove a few shreds of the rind from the lime for decoration, then cut the lime in half and squeeze out the juice.

4 Place the lime juice in a small saucepan with the lemon grass and sugar. Heat gently without boiling until the sugar is completely dissolved. Remove the saucepan from the heat and leave to cool completely.

5 Sieve the cooled syrup into a small jug and pour evenly over the mango slices.

6 Sprinkle with the lime rind strips, cover and leave to chill in the refrigerator before serving. Serve chilled.

221

mango with sticky rice

serves four

225 g/8 oz glutinous rice, soaked
    for 30 minutes in cold water
250 ml/9 fl oz coconut milk
2 tbsp caster sugar
pinch of salt
2 large ripe mangoes

1 Drain the rice and rinse thoroughly. Place in a saucepan with the coconut milk, sugar and salt. Bring to the boil and simmer, stirring occasionally, until the rice has absorbed all the coconut milk and is very soft.

2 Transfer the rice to a steamer set over a saucepan of simmering water. Cover and steam for 15 minutes. Leave to cool slightly. Press the rice into the base of 4 ramekins and turn out on to individual plates to form rice domes. Alternatively, spread the rice out on a tray lined with foil, then roll the rice flat with a wet rolling pin. Cut into diamond shapes.

3 Peel the mangoes and cut the flesh into cubes. Arrange the rice diamonds and mango cubes on individual plates or in ramekin dishes and serve.

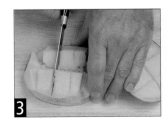

222

exotic fruit salad

serves six

1 tsp jasmine tea

1 tsp grated fresh root ginger

juice of 1 lime plus 1 strip of
   lime rind

125 ml/4 fl oz boiling water

2 tbsp caster sugar

1 pawpaw

1 mango

½ small pineapple

1 starfruit

2 passion fruit

COOK'S TIP

Starfruit have little flavour when unripe and green, but once ripened and yellow they become delicately sweet and fragrant. Usually by this stage, the tips of the ridges have become brown, so you will need to remove these before slicing. The easiest and quickest method of doing this is to run a vegetable peeler along each ridge.

3

4

5

1 Place the tea, ginger and lime rind in a heatproof jug and pour over the boiling water. Leave to infuse for 5 minutes, then sieve the liquid.

2 Add the sugar to the liquid and stir well to dissolve. Leave the syrup until it is completely cold.

3 Halve, deseed and peel the pawpaw. Halve the mango, remove the stone and peel. Peel and remove the core from the pineapple. Cut the fruits into bite-sized pieces.

4 Slice the starfruit crossways. Place all the prepared fruits in a wide serving bowl and pour over the cooled syrup. Cover with clingfilm and leave to chill in the refrigerator for 1 hour.

5 Cut the passion fruit in half, scoop out the flesh with a teaspoon and mix with the lime juice. Spoon over the salad and serve.

tropical fruit in lemon grass syrup

serves four

1 honeydew melon

1 small pineapple

1 pawpaw

400 g/14 oz lychees, stoned

3 passion fruit

LEMON GRASS SYRUP

150 g/5½ oz caster sugar

150 ml/5 fl oz water

2 lemon grass stalks, bruised

2 fresh kaffir lime leaves

juice of 1 lime

TO DECORATE

1 tbsp lime rind

small handful of fresh mint leaves

VARIATION

If fresh lychees are unavailable, replace them with drained canned ones.

1 To make the syrup, place all the ingredients in a saucepan. Heat gently until the sugar has dissolved. Bring to the boil and cook, uncovered, for 5 minutes. Leave to stand overnight.

2 Cut the melon in half, remove the seeds and scoop out the flesh with a melon baller. Place in a bowl. Peel the pineapple, cut into quarters lengthways and remove the core. Cut into cubes and add to the melon. Peel the pawpaw, remove the seeds and cut the flesh into cubes, then add to the other fruit.

3 Add the lychees. Cut the passion fruit in half and scoop the pulp and seeds into the bowl of fruit. Stir to mix, then transfer to a serving bowl. Remove the lemon grass and lime leaves from the syrup and pour over the fruit. Decorate with the lime rind and mint leaves and serve.

224

mango & lime sorbet

serves four

85 g/3 oz caster sugar

100 ml/3½ fl oz water

finely grated rind of 3 limes

2 tbsp coconut cream

2 large ripe mangoes

9 tbsp lime juice

curls of fresh coconut, toasted,
to decorate

VARIATION

If you prefer, canned mangoes in syrup can be used to make the sorbet. Omit the sugar and water, and infuse the lime rind in the canned syrup instead.

1 Place the sugar, water and lime rind in a small saucepan and heat gently, stirring constantly, until the sugar dissolves. Boil rapidly for 2 minutes to reduce slightly, then remove the saucepan from the heat and sieve into a heatproof bowl or jug. Stir in the coconut cream and cool.

2 Halve the mangoes, remove the stones and peel thinly. Chop the flesh roughly and place in a food processor with the lime juice. Process to a smooth purée and transfer to a small bowl.

3 Pour the cooled syrup into the mango purée, mixing evenly. Tip into a large, freezerproof container and freeze for 1 hour, or until slushy in texture. Alternatively, use an ice cream machine.

4 Remove the container from the freezer and beat with an electric mixer to break up the ice crystals. Refreeze for a further 1 hour, then remove from the freezer and beat the contents again until smooth.

5 Cover the container, return to the freezer and leave until firm. To serve, remove from the freezer and leave at room temperature for 15 minutes before scooping into individual glass dishes. Sprinkle with toasted coconut, to decorate.

rose ice

serves four

400 ml/14 fl oz water

2 tbsp coconut cream

4 tbsp sweetened condensed milk

2 tsp rosewater

few drops of pink food colouring
   (optional)

pink rose petals, to decorate

1 Place the water in a small saucepan and add the coconut cream. Heat the mixture gently without boiling, stirring.

2 Remove the saucepan from the heat and leave to cool. Stir in the condensed milk, rosewater and food colouring, if using.

3 Pour the mixture into a large, freezerproof container and freeze for 1–1½ hours, or until slushy.

4 Remove the container from the freezer and break up the ice crystals with a fork. Return to the freezer and freeze until firm.

5 Spoon the ice roughly into a pile on a serving dish and sprinkle with rose petals to serve.

COOK'S TIP
To prevent the ice thawing too quickly at the table, nestle the base of the serving dish in another dish filled with crushed ice.

228

easy mango ice cream

**makes about 1 litre
or 1½ pints**

600 ml/1 pint ready-made
traditional custard

150 ml/5 fl oz whipping cream,
lightly whipped

flesh of 2 ripe mangoes, puréed

icing sugar, to taste

passion fruit pulp, to serve

1 Mix the custard, cream and
mango purée together in a bowl.

2 Taste for sweetness and, if
necessary, add icing sugar to
taste, remembering that when frozen,
the mixture will taste less sweet.

3 Transfer the mixture to a large,
freezerproof container. Cover and
freeze for 2–3 hours, or until just
frozen. Spoon into a bowl and mash
with a fork or whisk to break down any
ice crystals. Return the mixture to the
container and freeze for a further
2 hours. Mash once more, then freeze
for 2–3 hours, or until firm.

4 Transfer the ice cream from
the freezer to the refrigerator
20–30 minutes before serving. Serve
with the passion fruit pulp.

229

lychee & ginger sorbet

serves four

800 g/1 lb 12 oz canned lychees
    in syrup
finely grated rind of 1 lime
2 tbsp lime juice
3 tbsp stem ginger syrup
2 egg whites
TO DECORATE
starfruit slices
slivers of stem ginger

1 Drain the lychees, reserving the syrup. Place the lychees in a food processor or blender with the lime rind, juice and stem ginger syrup and process until completely smooth. Transfer to a large bowl.

COOK'S TIP

It is not recommended that raw eggs are served to very young children, pregnant women, the elderly or anyone weakened by chronic illness. The egg whites may be left out of this recipe, but you will need to whisk the sorbet a second time after a further 1 hour of freezing to obtain a light texture.

2 Mix the purée thoroughly with the reserved lychee syrup, then pour into a large, freezerproof container and freeze for 1–1½ hours, or until slushy in texture. Alternatively, use an ice cream machine.

3 Remove from the freezer and whisk to break up the ice crystals. Whisk the egg whites in a clean, dry bowl until stiff, then quickly and lightly fold into the iced mixture.

4 Return to the freezer and leave until firm. Serve the sorbet in scoops, with slices of starfruit and slivers of ginger to decorate.

coconut & ginger ice cream

makes about 1 litre
or 1½ pints

400 ml/14 fl oz coconut milk

250 ml/9 fl oz whipping cream

4 egg yolks

5 tbsp caster sugar

4 tbsp stem ginger syrup

6 pieces stem ginger, finely
chopped

2 tbsp lime juice

fresh mint sprigs, to decorate

TO SERVE

lychees

preserved ginger syrup

1 Place the coconut milk and cream in a saucepan. Heat gently until just beginning to simmer. Remove the saucepan from the heat.

2 Beat the egg yolks, sugar and ginger syrup together in a large bowl until pale and creamy. Slowly pour in the hot coconut milk mixture, while stirring. Return to the saucepan and heat gently, stirring constantly, until the mixture thickens and coats the back of a spoon. Remove the saucepan from the heat and leave to cool. Stir in the ginger and lime juice.

3 Transfer the mixture to a large, freezerproof container. Cover and freeze for 2–3 hours, or until just frozen. Spoon into a bowl and mash with a fork or whisk to break down any ice crystals. Return the mixture to the container and freeze for a further 2 hours. Mash once more, then freeze for 2–3 hours, or until firm.

4 Transfer to the refrigerator 20–30 minutes before serving. Decorate with mint sprigs and serve with lychees and a little ginger syrup drizzled over.

231

pineapple with cardamom & lime

serves four

1 pineapple

2 cardamom pods

thinly pared lime rind

4 tbsp water

1 tbsp soft light brown sugar

3 tbsp lime juice

TO DECORATE

fresh mint sprigs

whipped cream

COOK'S TIP

To remove the 'eyes' from
pineapple, cut off the peel, then
use a small sharp knife to cut a
V-shaped channel down the
pineapple, cutting diagonally
through the lines of brown 'eyes'
in the flesh, to make spiralling
cuts around the fruit.

1 Cut the top and base from the
pineapple, cut away the peel and
remove the 'eyes' from the flesh (see
Cook's Tip). Cut into quarters and
remove the core. Slice the pineapple
lengthways and place in a large
serving dish.

2 Crush the cardamom pods in a
mortar using a pestle and mortar
and place in a saucepan with the lime
rind and the water. Bring to the boil,
then reduce the heat and simmer for
30 seconds.

3 Remove the saucepan from the
heat and add the sugar, then
cover with a lid and leave to infuse for
5 minutes.

4 Stir in the sugar to dissolve, add
the lime juice, then sieve the
syrup over the pineapple. Cover and
chill in the refrigerator for 30 minutes.

5 When ready to serve, decorate
with mint sprigs and a spoonful
of whipped cream.

mung bean custards

serves six

125 g/4½ oz dried mung beans

2 eggs, beaten

175 ml/6 fl oz coconut milk

100 g/3½ oz caster sugar

1 tbsp ground rice

1 tsp ground cinnamon, plus extra
 for sprinkling

butter, for greasing

TO DECORATE

crème fraîche or whipped cream

finely grated lime rind

sliced starfruit

pomegranate seeds

1 Preheat the oven to 180°C/350°F/
 Gas Mark 4. Place the dried mung
beans in a saucepan with enough
water to cover. Bring to the boil,
then reduce the heat and simmer for
30–40 minutes, until the beans are
very tender. Drain well.

COOK'S TIP
To save time, use canned mung
beans. Drain the beans
thoroughly, mash and purée and
add to the bowl with the eggs
and coconut milk.

2 Mash the beans, then press
 through a sieve to form a smooth
purée. Place the bean purée, eggs,
coconut milk, sugar, ground rice and
cinnamon in a large bowl and beat
well until mixed.

3 Grease and line the base of
 4 x 150-ml/5-fl oz pudding-
shaped moulds or ramekin dishes and
pour in the mixture. Place on a baking
sheet in the preheated oven and bake
for 20–25 minutes, or until just set.

4 Leave the custards to cool in
 the moulds, then run a knife
around the edges to loosen and turn
out on to individual serving plates.
Sprinkle with cinnamon. Decorate with
crème fraîche, lime rind, starfruit and
pomegranate seeds.

balinese banana pancakes

serves six

175 g/6 oz plain flour

pinch of salt

4 eggs, beaten

2 large ripe bananas, mashed

300 ml/10 fl oz coconut milk

vegetable oil, for frying

coconut cream, to serve

TO DECORATE

sliced banana

6 tbsp lime juice

icing sugar

1 Place the flour, salt, eggs, bananas and coconut milk in a food processor or blender and process to a smooth batter. Alternatively, sift the flour and salt into a bowl and make a well in the centre, then add the remaining ingredients and beat well until smooth.

2 Leave the batter to chill in the refrigerator for 1 hour. Remove the batter from the refrigerator and beat briefly again. Heat a small amount of oil in a small frying pan until very hot.

3 Drop tablespoonfuls of the batter into the frying pan. Cook until the pancakes are golden underneath.

4 Turn over and cook the other sides until golden brown. Cook in batches until all the batter is used up, making 36 pancakes. Remove and leave to drain on kitchen paper.

5 Arrange the pancakes in a stack, layered with sliced bananas, sprinkled with lime juice and icing sugar and served with coconut cream.

caramel apple wedges with sesame seeds

serves four

115 g/4 oz rice flour

1 egg

125 ml/4 fl oz cold water

4 crisp dessert apples

2½ tbsp sesame seeds

250 g/9 oz caster sugar

2 tbsp vegetable oil, plus extra for
    deep-frying

fresh basil sprigs, to decorate

1 Place the flour, egg and water in a large bowl and whisk well until a smooth, thick batter forms.

2 Core the apples and cut each into 8 wedges. Drop into the batter and stir in the sesame seeds.

3 Place the sugar and the 2 tablespoons of oil in a heavy-based frying pan and heat, stirring, until the sugar dissolves. Continue until the syrup begins to turn golden. Remove the frying pan from the heat but keep warm.

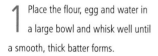

COOK'S TIP

Take care not to overheat the sugar syrup, otherwise it will become difficult to handle and burn. If it begins to set before you have finished dipping the apple pieces, warm it slightly until it becomes liquid again.

4 Heat the oil for deep-frying in a deep frying pan or wok to 180–190°C/350–375°F, or until a cube of bread browns in 30 seconds. Lift the apple pieces one by one from the batter using tongs, lower into the hot oil and deep-fry for 2–3 minutes, or until golden brown and crisp.

5 Remove with a slotted spoon and dip very quickly into the sugar mixture. Dip the apple wedges briefly into a bowl of iced water and drain on kitchen paper. Transfer to a serving plate, decorate with basil and serve immediately.

banana fritters in coconut batter

serves four

70 g/2½ oz plain flour

2 tbsp rice flour

1 tbsp caster sugar

1 egg, separated

150 ml/5 fl oz coconut milk

sunflower oil, for deep-frying

4 large bananas

TO DECORATE

1 tsp icing sugar

1 tsp ground cinnamon

lime wedges

COOK'S TIP

If you can buy the baby finger bananas that are popular in this dish in the East, leave them whole for coating and frying.

1 Sift the plain flour, rice flour and sugar into a bowl and make a well in the centre. Add the egg yolk and coconut milk.

2 Beat the mixture until a smooth, thick batter forms. Whisk the egg white in a clean, dry bowl until stiff soft peaks form then fold it into the batter lightly and evenly.

3 Heat 6-cm/2½-inch of oil in a large frying pan to 180–190°C/350–375°F, or until a cube of bread browns in 30 seconds. Cut the bananas in half crossways, then dip them quickly into the batter to coat them.

4 Drop the bananas carefully into the hot oil and fry in batches for 2–3 minutes, until golden brown, turning once.

5 Drain on kitchen paper. Sprinkle with icing sugar and cinnamon and decorate with lime wedges.

coconut pancakes

serves four

115 g/4 oz rice flour

40 g/1½ oz caster sugar

pinch of salt

2 eggs

600 ml/1 pint coconut milk

4 tbsp desiccated coconut

vegetable oil, for frying

2 tbsp palm sugar, for sprinkling

fresh mango or banana, to serve

1 Place the rice flour, caster sugar and salt in a bowl and add the eggs and coconut milk. Whisk until a smooth batter forms. Alternatively, place all the ingredients in a food processor or blender and process to a smooth batter. Beat in half the coconut.

2 Heat a small amount of oil in a wide, heavy-based frying pan. Pour in a little batter, swirling the frying pan to cover the surface thinly and evenly. Cook until the pancake is pale golden underneath.

3 Turn the pancake and cook quickly to brown lightly on the other side.

4 Remove the pancake from the frying pan and keep hot while using the remaining batter to make a total of 8 pancakes.

5 Lightly toast the remaining coconut and reserve. Transfer the pancakes folded or loosely rolled to serving plates, sprinkle with palm sugar and the toasted coconut and serve with slices of mango or banana.

crêpes with pawpaw & passion fruit

serves four

2 eggs

125 ml/4 fl oz coconut milk

175 ml/6 fl oz milk

115 g/4 oz plain flour

pinch of salt

1 tbsp caster sugar

15 g/$\frac{1}{2}$ oz butter, melted

oil, for frying

sifted icing sugar, for dusting

FILLING

2 pawpaw

3 passion fruit

juice of 1 lime

2 tbsp icing sugar

COOK'S TIP

To enjoy these crêpes at their very best serve this dessert as soon as it has been assembled.

1 Whisk the eggs, coconut milk and milk together in a bowl. Sift the flour and salt into a separate bowl. Stir in the caster sugar. Make a well in the centre of the flour and gradually beat in the egg mixture to form a smooth batter. Stir in the melted butter.

2 Heat a 20–23-cm/8–9-inch non-stick frying pan and brush with oil. Pour in enough batter to coat the base. Tip the frying pan as you pour it in, so the base is evenly coated. Cook until browned on the underside and set on top, then turn the crêpe over and cook the other side. Place on a plate, cover with foil and keep warm while making the remaining crêpes.

3 Peel the pawpaw, cut in half and scoop out the seeds, reserving a few. Cut into chunks and place in a bowl. Cut the passion fruit in half and scoop the seeds and pulp into the bowl. Stir in the lime juice and icing sugar. Put a little filling on one-quarter of each crêpe. Fold in half and then into quarters. Dust with sifted icing sugar. Sprinkle the reserved pawpaw seeds over and serve at once.

240

coconut custard squares

serves four

1 tsp butter, melted

6 eggs

400 ml/14 fl oz coconut milk

175 g/6 oz soft light brown sugar

pinch of salt

fresh fruit slices, to serve

TO DECORATE

shreds of coconut

strips of lime rind

COOK'S TIP

Keep an eye on the custard as it bakes, because if it overcooks, the texture will be spoiled. When the custard comes out of the oven, it should be barely set and still slightly wobbly in the centre. It will firm up slightly as it cools.

1 Preheat the oven to 180°C/350°F/ Gas Mark 4. Brush the melted butter over the inside of a 19-cm/ 7½-inch square ovenproof dish, about 4 cm/1½ inch in depth.

2 Beat the eggs in a large bowl, then beat in the coconut milk, sugar and salt.

3 Place the bowl over a saucepan of gently simmering water and stir with a wooden spoon for 15 minutes, or until it begins to thicken. Pour into the prepared dish.

4 Bake in the preheated oven for 20–25 minutes, until just set. Remove the dish from the oven and leave to cool completely.

5 Turn the custard out of the dish and cut into squares. Serve decorated with coconut shreds and lime rind together with slices of fruit.

bananas in coconut milk

serves four

4 large bananas

350 ml/12 fl oz coconut milk

2 tbsp caster sugar

pinch of salt

1 tsp orange flower water

1 tbsp shredded fresh mint

2 tbsp cooked mung beans

fresh mint sprigs, to decorate

1 Peel the bananas and cut them into short chunks. Place in a large saucepan with the coconut milk, sugar and salt.

2 Heat gently until boiling and simmer for 1 minute. Remove the saucepan from the heat.

3 Sprinkle the orange flower water over the banana mixture, stir in the mint and spoon into a serving dish.

4 Place the mung beans in a heavy-based frying pan and cook over a high heat until they turn crisp and golden, shaking the frying pan occasionally. Leave the beans to cool slightly, then crush lightly in a mortar using a pestle.

5 Sprinkle the toasted beans over the bananas and serve warm or cold, decorated with mint sprigs.

sticky rice shapes

serves four

300 g/10½ oz glutinous rice

500 g/1 lb 2 oz granulated sugar

300 ml/10 fl oz water

few drops of rosewater or
    jasmine essence

pink and green food colourings

rose petals or jasmine flowers,
    to decorate

1 Place the rice in a bowl and add enough cold water to cover. Leave to soak for 3 hours or overnight.

2 Drain the rice and rinse thoroughly in cold water. Line the top part of a steamer with muslin and tip the rice into it. Place over boiling water, then cover and steam for 30 minutes. Remove the rice from the steamer and leave to cool.

3 Heat the sugar and water gently in a saucepan until the sugar dissolves. Add the rosewater. Bring to the boil and boil for 4–5 minutes to reduce to a thin syrup. Remove the saucepan from the heat.

4 Divide the rice in half and colour one half pale pink, the other half pale green. Form into small balls or shapes using moulds (see Cook's Tip).

5 Using 2 forks, dip the rice shapes into the syrup. Drain off the excess syrup and pile on to a dish. Decorate with rose petals or jasmine flowers and serve.

COOK'S TIP

If you prefer, the rice can be shaped in small sweet moulds or dariole moulds to produce small castle or turret shapes.

244

coconut cake with lime & ginger syrup

serves four

2 large eggs, separated

pinch of salt

100 g/3½ oz caster sugar

75 g/2¾ oz butter, melted
   and cooled

5 tbsp coconut milk

150 g/5½ oz self-raising flour

½ tsp baking powder

3 tbsp desiccated coconut

4 tbsp stem ginger syrup

3 tbsp lime juice

TO DECORATE

3 pieces stem ginger

curls of fresh coconut

finely grated lime rind

1 Cut a 28-cm/11-inch round of baking paper and press into an 18-cm/7-inch steamer basket to line it.

2 Whisk the egg whites with the salt in a clean, dry bowl until stiff. Gradually whisk in the sugar, 1 tablespoon at a time, whisking hard after each addition until the mixture forms stiff peaks.

3 Whisk in the yolks, then quickly stir in the butter and coconut milk. Sift the flour and baking powder over the mixture, then fold in lightly and evenly with a large metal spoon. Fold in the coconut.

4 Spoon the mixture into the lined steamer basket and tuck the spare paper over the top. Place the basket over boiling water, cover and steam for 30 minutes.

5 Transfer the cake to a plate, remove the paper and leave to cool slightly. Mix the ginger syrup and lime juice together and spoon over the cake. Cut into squares and decorate with pieces of stem ginger, curls of coconut and lime rind.

246

melon & ginger crush

serves four

1 melon, about 800 g/1 lb 12 oz

6 tbsp ginger wine

3 tbsp kaffir lime juice or lime juice

crushed ice

1 lime

1 Peel, deseed and roughly chop the melon. Place the melon in a food processor or blender with the ginger wine and lime juice.

4 Cut the lime into thin slices, cut a slit in 4 of the slices and slip one on to the side of each glass. Add the remaining slices of lime to each glass, then serve immediately.

2 Blend together on high speed until the melon mixture is smooth.

3 Place plenty of crushed ice in 4 tall glasses. Pour the melon and ginger crush over the ice.

VARIATION

If you prefer a non-alcoholic version of this drink, simply omit the ginger wine, then top up with ginger ale in the glass. For a change of flavour, use a watermelon when they are in season. Ginger wine is available from specialist wine merchants.

248

tropical fruit punch

serves six

1 small ripe mango

4 tbsp lime juice

1 tsp finely grated fresh root ginger

1 tbsp soft light brown sugar

300 ml/10 fl oz orange juice

300 ml/10 fl oz pineapple juice

100 ml/3½ fl oz rum

crushed ice

TO DECORATE

orange slices

lime slices

pineapple slices

starfruit slices

1 Peel and stone the mango and chop the flesh. Place in a food processor or blender with the lime juice, ginger and sugar and process until smooth.

2 Add the orange and pineapple juices, then add the rum and process again for a few seconds until blended. Divide the crushed ice between 6 glasses and pour the punch over the ice.

3 Add the orange and lime slices, then arrange the pineapple and starfruit slices on the rim of each glass. Serve immediately.

lime & lemon grass cooler

serves four

egg white

3 tbsp caster sugar, plus extra
for frosting

2 limes

1 small lemon grass stalk

4 ice cubes

125 ml/4 fl oz water

4 lime slices

soda water

1 To frost the rims of the glasses, pour a little egg white into a saucer. Spread a small amount of sugar out on a plate. Dip the rim of each glass briefly into the egg white, then into the sugar.

2 Cut each lime into 8 pieces and roughly chop the lemon grass. Place the lime pieces and lemon grass in a food processor or blender with the sugar and ice cubes.

3 Add the water and process for a few seconds. Try not to overprocess, otherwise the drink will have a bitter flavour.

4 Sieve the mixture into the frosted glasses. Add a lime slice to each glass and top up with soda water to taste. Serve immediately.

250

mango & coconut smoothie

serves four

2 large ripe mangoes

1 tbsp icing sugar

500 ml/18 fl oz coconut milk

5 ice cubes

flaked, toasted coconut, to serve

1 Using a sharp knife, cut the mangoes in half and remove the stone. Peel and roughly chop the flesh.

2 Place the chopped flesh in a food processor or blender with the icing sugar and process until completely smooth.

COOK'S TIP
To add a special kick to this drink, add a generous dash of white rum to the blender or food processor with the coconut milk.

3 Add the coconut milk and ice cubes to the blender or food processor and process until frothy.

4 Pour into 4 tall glasses and sprinkle with flaked, toasted coconut to serve.

VARIATION
If you don't have flaked, toasted coconut, sprinkle with ground ginger, cinnamon or nutmeg just before serving.

thai cocktail sling

serves one

2 tbsp whisky

1 tbsp cherry brandy

1 tbsp orange-flavoured liqueur

1 tbsp lime juice

1 tsp palm sugar

dash of Angostura bitters

2 ice cubes

125 ml/4 fl oz pineapple juice

1 small pineapple wedge

1 Place the whisky, cherry brandy, liqueur, lime juice, sugar and Angostura bitters in a cocktail shaker. Shake well to mix thoroughly.

2 Place the ice cubes in a large glass. Pour the cocktail mixture over the ice, then top up with the pineapple juice.

3 Cut a slit in the pineapple wedge and arrange on the edge of the glass. Serve immediately.

COOK'S TIP

If the pineapple juice is quite sweet, as Thai pineapple juice is, you may not need to add sugar. So if you're unsure, taste first. Scotch whisky is very highly regarded in Thailand, although a powerful whisky is distilled locally – if you have the stomach for it!

252